More praise for
TAKE IT TO THE NEXT LEVEL

"*Take It to the Next Level* points out a truth that is disappearing from the American workplace. That truth is that perfection in producing a quality product is the result of hard work, determination, and cohesiveness between management and employees. I admire Dale Crownover for his truthfulness in writing about his quest for zero defects and the personal insight he gained during his journey. This book could provide the basis for teaching classes on work ethic and attaining a dream in today's industrial climate. Crownover deserves congratulations for this honest book and for making Texas Nameplate a real winner!"

Representative Jim Pitts
House of Representatives
State of Texas

"A unique leadership testament, *Take It to the Next Level* combines both a personal and organizational journey to excellence. Over and over again, I found the book both heart-warming and educational."

Vic Sassone, Executive Director
The Hogan Center
for Performance Excellence

TAKE IT
TO THE
NEXT LEVEL

A STORY OF THE
QUEST FOR QUALITY
AND THE
MALCOLM BALDRIGE AWARD

BY

DALE CROWNOVER

WITH

LINDA BUSH
AND
JOHN DARROUZET

TAKE IT TO THE NEXT LEVEL

A STORY OF THE
QUEST FOR QUALITY
AND THE
MALCOLM BALDRIGE AWARD

by
Dale Crownover
with
Linda Bush and John Darrouzet

Published by
NextLevel Press
2915 LBJ Freeway
Suite 152
Dallas, Texas 75234-7607

ISBN 0-9667519-0-6

THANK GOD FOR
THOSE WHO
BRUNG YOU.

TABLE OF CONTENTS

TAKE IT TO THE NEXT LEVEL

APPENDIX

Acknowledgments

I know of no sport, business, or political success that could be attained without the aid of other individuals. A leader is responsible for inspiring a dream, acknowledging the people who participated, and encouraging them to pursue their dreams.

Our company produces identification plates that provide product information. What is significant about our company is our people. This book was possible because of their desire, determination and commitment to make the company better, not bigger. I thank them wholeheartedly for having faith and confidence in my decisions, vision, and goals.

Writing the Baldrige application and this book were two major challenges for someone who can tell but not write a story. I appreciate Jackie Kennett, Bruce Beede, and Barry Johnson for their time and patience with the Baldrige journey. I thank John Darrouzet, Linda Bush, and Warren Hogan for the endless hours and their confidence in me to write this book. Heartfelt thanks to our consulting editors Francena Hancock and Lynne Darrouzet. And we couldn't tell our tale without the capable assistance of Sula Reilly who created the charts.

As my dad taught me, I appreciate all the loving spouses and families who helped us all to *Take It to the Next Level*.

Dale Crownover
Dallas, October 1998

DEDICATION

This book is dedicated to:

the Employees* of
Texas Nameplate Company, Inc.

my parents
Roy Douglas Crownover
and
Bernyce Ewing Crownover

my wife
Julie Lee Crownover

my children
Ryan Dale and Roy Dan
Crownover

(* I'm proud to name the people who
journeyed with me on page 209.)

FOREWORD

South of downtown, in a less affluent part of Dallas, a small miracle has been quietly but steadily unfolding over the last few years. Dale Crownover, president and chief miracle worker of Texas Nameplate Company, and his spirited band of 63 employees have reinvented and re-shaped the company in an extraordinary way.

From former days of massive employee turn-over, high scrap rates, and lackluster attention to customers, this small manufacturing com-pany is now SPC- and TQM-fluent to a degree that is the envy of larger corporations. This is a turnaround story whose very simplicity will at once dazzle you and stir your emotions.

Winner of a growing number of prestigious awards, Texas Nameplate shows no signs of easing up on its efforts to achieve industry pre-eminence in product quality, customer focus, and care for employees.

In this unique account of a remarkable symbio-sis between leadership and followership, the humble Crownover readily attributes the com-pany's success to his employees' talents and adaptability to change.

In telling the story of his quality journey, Dale has had the courage to reveal his anxieties and insecurities all along the way. This gives en-couragement to those of us who face similar demons as we try to "take it to the next level."

His homespun philosophy and aw-shucks persona are real, endearing and effective in getting the job done. Moreover, he is a good friend to those of us fortunate enough to get to know him.

I recommend you read his compelling story … and become better prepared for your own particular humbling experience.

Robert D. McTeer
President & CEO
Federal Reserve Bank of Dallas

PREFACE

Hi, I'm Warren Hogan, Chairman of the Hogan Center. Let me briefly tell you why our Heart of American Business series starts with Dale Crownover's *Take It to the Next Level.*

It really begins back in 1982. I was in my nineteenth year with Texas Instruments as head of a $100 million division in Attleboro, Massachusetts. Like most of the semi-conductor industry, TI was competing intensely with the Japanese in the commercial and industrial electronics markets worldwide.

We were quite an arrogant company in those days, believing that we needed no outside assistance. However, TI did send its top 250 managers from all over the world to the Crosby College in Florida, where a large number of my colleagues missed the point. Fortunately, I returned to Attleboro with two profound insights: I was the biggest impediment to a serious breakthrough in quality in my division and my employees really could perform at or near "zero defects."

Later I heard Willis Willoughby, Deputy Chief of Naval Materials, describe his mission to dramatically improve the quality of the equipment and systems in the U.S. fleet. He hit on the deterioration of personal integrity, the need for caring, quality before quantity, and getting what you accept. I got it ... and my transformation was in full gear.

I soon left TI to become president of AirBorn, Inc., a Dallas electronic connector firm where I implemented a world-class, total quality system. In 1987 a growing AirBorn was named Motorola's Supplier of the Year, the same year Motorola won the Malcolm Baldrige National Quality Award.

Later in 1987, at an American Electronics Association breakfast meeting, Raymond Marlow, founder and CEO of Marlow Industries, asked how he could initiate a world-class performance excellence system. Sensing another career change, I sought the valuable input of my colleagues Mike Corboy, then president of Tocom, and Joe Mooibroek, then president of American Medical Electronics. We envisioned a "junior college" made up of groups of small and medium-sized companies who would collectively undergo a two-year implementation of performance excellence principles. I became "Professor Hogan" and the Hogan Center was created. Raymond Marlow was our first enrollee and led his company to receive the Malcolm Baldrige National Quality Award in 1991.

To date, the Hogan Center has worked with over a hundred small and medium-sized organizations toward the goal of achieving performance excellence. Four of the eight winners of the Texas Quality Award in the last three years are members of our Center. One of these is Texas Nameplate whose passionate leader, Dale Crownover, describes in this book his journey to "take it to the next level".

What makes this story so unique is how Dale overcame tremendous personal and business obstacles to lead his small second-generation, family-owned company to world-class recognition.

Dale's story proves that, when organizations develop people's skills, increase their involvement in problem solving, and provide them ownership of their processes, the results are better products and service for their customers and the rewards of increased business. The pride, excitement, fulfillment and motivation that spills into these employees' lives, with increased self-esteem, personal achievement, and renewed integrity inevitably affects their families and communities. In the broader view, the creation of this environment strengthens America and ultimately the world.

Reading this book may spark for you a transformation like mine in 1982. Your desire, determination and commitment can lead others on a journey to compete with the world's best and, in the process, to learn, grow and give.

Warren Hogan, Chairman
Hogan Center
for Performance Excellence

TAKE IT
TO THE
NEXT LEVEL

 **PROLOGUE**

In January of 1998, I got a call from my friend Warren Hogan, Chairman of the Hogan Center for Performance Excellence. He said he had an idea he wanted to talk to me about in person and asked if he could come down to my office. I said sure and he drove down.

Warren is one of those executives that likes to get right to the point and he did. He said he wanted to know if we were ready to tell the story of Texas Nameplate Company, of the journey we had taken over the last eight years as we entered the competition for the Texas Quality and the Malcolm Baldrige Awards.

At first I was not clear on his meaning. I thought he wanted to hear me give him an executive summary of who and what we were, where we had come from and where we thought we were going. He listened patiently as I briefly reviewed our history.

First I told him that Texas Nameplate Company was a small company born just after World War II. That war had brought a demand for military defense equipment such as tanks, trucks, airplanes, ships, artillery, etc. All of these items required identification and information plates that could withstand adverse conditions on land, sea, and in the air. The need for manufacturers of etched metal processes was born.

Companies involved in the photo-engraving process for the paper printing industry were recruited by the War Department to produce etched metal nameplates for the many companies involved in the war effort.

Then I reminded Warren that in 1946, after the war was over, Charles Steineger, Tom Hampton, and my father Roy Crownover founded and began the operation of Texas Nameplate Company. The company grew from those three employees to over 100 in the 1980s.

Because of new equipment, new techniques, and an excellent quality control program, I told him we now needed only 63 employees to produce more quality nameplates than ever before.

Then Warren interrupted me with some impatience.

He said he knew what Texas Nameplate was, its history, that it was a customer-oriented, family-owned business serving the private sector, and that it was committed to total quality management. He knew that we manufacture the identification labels commonly seen on all types of products — from refrigerators to high-pressure valves to computer equipment. He knew our nameplates are used for identification and to inform end-users of electronic and computer equipment, oilfield equipment, valves, pressure vessels, and vehicles.

He said that while it was important for more businesses to know about what we did and that the information on nameplates may be critical — serial numbers, model numbers, pressure limits, vendor names, installation procedures, safety warnings, etc. — he was not asking me to tell those kinds of stories. He was not asking me to tell how our nameplate information helps identify potentially dangerous situations to users throughout the life of the product or provides important product information not generally found anywhere else.

In other words he was not asking for a marketing story.

He said he was sure that engineers might find it fascinating to learn about the techniques used to manufacture nameplates including screen printing, photo engraving, and chemical etching. But he was after something else.

He wanted to know if I was ready to tell the Texas Nameplate story that might really matter to small-business men and women across the United States. Since it appeared he knew our story better than we did, I asked him to tell me what he had in mind.

Warren smiled like I had finally given him the go-ahead to say his prepared script.

"What I'm interested in," he said, "is how a small business like Texas Nameplate, with its employee force of 63 people, with an average age of 42, could be competing for the Malcolm Baldrige National Quality Award, thinking it might be anywhere close to winning." He looked me straight in the eye. Like the precise corporate executive I knew him to be, he riveted me with five, well-chosen words:

"What drives you to compete?"

Now, Warren had heard about how closely knit an organization we are. We have excellent internal communication and a strong sense of personal ownership in the quality of our manufactured products. Many of our employees have grown up with the company and have a genuine stake in the company's profitability and continued success.

I'd been around Warren for several years and I knew that the mission of the Hogan Center for Performance Excellence involves a sincere desire to strengthen America. Since I agreed with that mission, since we are friends, and since he'd come all the way across Dallas to urge me to tell our story, I felt obliged to respond, then and there.

I pulled out some work papers from a file drawer and paused briefly as I remembered the hard work we had put into our Baldrige application.

Then I told him I had some "good news" and "bad news." I asked him which he wanted to hear first. "Give me the bad news first," he said. "Then there'll be something to look forward to."

"The bad news, Warren," I began, "is that I can tell you what drives Texas Nameplate in less than five minutes." He looked puzzled, but didn't skip a beat. He wanted what he came for and was determined to get it.

So, as Warren began to jot them down, I proceeded to tell him what was driving us to be so successful. I told him how we had come up with seven "key business drivers" at Texas

Nameplate. He asked what they were and I summarized them as follows:

1. Customer Satisfaction
This first driver helps us measure the quality of our products by the level of satisfaction our customers experience with them.

2. Employee Satisfaction
This second driver helps us measure the quality of our employees by the level of satisfaction they experience while making our products.

3. Environmental Consciousness
Warren asked me to explain this third driver a bit, since it wasn't as obvious as the first two.

I told him that, given the hazardous waste that may be produced in our etching processes, we had to be very conscious of what we may be doing to the environment at all times.

I smiled remembering a childhood experience. I had spilled a whole tray of type Julian Ramirez was using in the Art Department. Thousands of pieces went all over the floor. He just looked at me and said he would clean it up. I said I was sorry and left in a hurry.

I told Warren that as adults in the workplace and in our community, we had to prepare for spills and be ready to clean up after ourselves. This third driver helps us measure the quality of our product's impact on our community.

4. Fair Profit

Our fourth driver for Texas Nameplate is achieving a fair profit for the work we do. I explained that the approach we have developed, not only in the pricing of our products and services, but also in our wages, profit-sharing, gain-sharing, and employee benefits had proven to be truly outstanding.

5. Controlled Growth

We call our fifth driver controlled growth. It is Texas Nameplate's planned effort to grow, but not to grow too big nor too fast. It helps us measure the quality and proportions of our growth internally and in our market. Warren asked me to elaborate on this one a bit too.

I told him that we have all learned that if we do not respect what we have at Texas Nameplate, we will surely risk losing it. We respect what we are capable of doing, individually and as a team. We also respect what we are not yet capable of doing before we try to take the company to the next level.

As a result of controlled growth, our decision-making process is considerably more open. I emphasized that this driver may well be the key to our future.

6. Process Optimization

This sixth driver helps us measure the quality of our business processes so we can optimize our flow-through and our outputs. Since the quality of our products is the direct result of how we process our materials, we do our best here.

7. External Interface

Our seventh driver, external interface, sounds more technical than it really is. It means we recognize the responsibility we have for giving back to the community in which we live and work. For Texas Nameplate this means South Dallas.

This driver helps us measure the quality of our relationship with our neighbors at Texas Nameplate. It is a way of fulfilling the age-old commandment to "love your neighbor as yourself."

We have adopted our neighborhood City Park Elementary School. We regularly work with the school administration to help meet the needs and desires of the school and the children it serves. We also share our story with other businesses through seminars, speeches, and articles.

Warren put the cap on his pen and closed his notebook. He realized he had gotten what he came for but was not really all that satisfied.

"If that's all that drives your business," he said, "why aren't more small-business men and women successful? I don't understand. You make it sound so simple."

"That's the bad news," I said. "It's so simple, many businesses miss what it takes to go to the next level."

"What does it take to go to the next level? What does it take to compete for the Malcolm Baldrige Award?" Warren asked.

I let his questions hang there for the moment and let our mutual silence fill the office.

Finally, Warren said, "So what's the 'good news' now that I'm stuck?"

"The 'good news' is that other small-business men and women don't have to know what drives Texas Nameplate to make their own businesses successful. The 'good news' is that they have to find out for themselves what drives them."

Warren was not a happy camper. "You mean to tell me that others won't learn from what you have been through on your quality journey?"

"No," I was quick to answer. "What I mean is that, if we were to tell them our story, they would have to realize ahead of time that we were not telling them how to make their own journey. They have to discover that for themselves. All we could do would be to tell them what it was like for us, how we hung in there, how we grew, what we learned...." I was getting excited just talking about the stories we could tell.

Warren smiled. "That's what I wanted to hear you say," he said.

"Yeah. Me too," I said.

That's when I knew that Warren, the Quality Crusader, and I had landed each other. We were both hooked by the prospect of telling the Texas Nameplate story.

So, in the pages that follow, I tell the story of our eight-year journey to change the way we conduct our family-owned business. At the heart of our story is what Warren was really after. He's a very good professional at helping people learn how to achieve quality.

But he's discovered like I have that knowing how to do a quality job is not as important as finding out why. Warren and I believe that if you first know why you want to go on the quest for quality, you'll find out how to do it as soon thereafter as possible.

Thus, this story is about why.

To introduce you to the story of Texas Nameplate, let me outline its contents. In the first chapter, "I Heard It on the Radio," you will learn about the ordinary concerns of one businessman who was just trying to keep it all going in the midst of a changing economy and an unexpected customer demand. In chapter two, "What Are They Talking About?" you will discover the issue that compelled my company to change. In chapter three, "No Way," I hope you will not only learn about, but really feel, the reluctance that came over me to take on the quest for quality. In chapter four, you may well find yourself asking, like I did, whether "Quality Is Free?"

In chapter five, "Some Fight, Some Flee, Some Surrender," you will have the opportunity to meet three distinct challenges we were being forced to deal with internally. In chapter six, "The Kitchen Was Hot," you will understand a bit of the heat that can be generated within a small business by internal friction over proposals to change. In chapter seven, "The Dark Before Dawn," I describe some of my own soul-searching about the "why" of it all. In chapter eight, "Z-D Day," you will get a glimpse of the "civil war" we endured. In chapter nine, "East Meets West," you will be introduced to the stranger who all but rescued us. He showed us why the quest for quality is one of the last real hopes for small businesses to survive into the future, in America or in the world.

In chapter 10, "Telling the Tale," I present the story of our quest for quality in terms that even bottom-liners will understand, like how we increased gross margins by 11 percentage points. In chapter 11, "Don't Kiss the Trophy," I recount our efforts to win the Texas Quality and Malcolm Baldrige Awards. And finally, in chapter 12, "Mr. Baldrige, Meet the Next Generation," I will give you my insights into why it is so significant to enter into such quality competitions.

At the end of this Prologue, you will find a timeline of important dates that will help you keep the time frames straight as the story unfolds.

I did not go on this journey alone — none of us who try it ever does. To demonstrate this I have included the voices of some of those who accompanied me along the way. At the end of each chapter, you will hear these voices so you will not be misled into thinking that the quest for quality can be accomplished single-handedly or without a shared vision.

In the *Appendix*, you will have the opportunity to see pictures of the quality leaders we have at Texas Nameplate and read a list of the people who make this journey possible.

Because there are some words I have used in telling the story that you may not be familiar with, I have included a *Glossary* for your reference.

If you find yourself wanting to learn more about the Malcolm Baldrige National Quality Award or your own state's quality program like the Texas Quality Award, I recommend that you visit the Texas Nameplate Company Internet Web site at www.nameplate.com or Warren's Web site for the Hogan Center for Performance Excellence at www.hogancenter.com. Both sites provide links to a growing list of quality-oriented Web sites.

If this story inspires you to read more about the quest for quality, I have also suggested a short list of books you might want to take a look at in the *Bibliography*.

Finally, I want to touch briefly on a subject that is very important to me, my family, and anyone else who chooses to go on the quest for quality.

The quest for quality can transform you in many different ways. For me, the most surprising transformation was the integration of my business goals and my religious faith.

As you will fairly quickly find out, I am by faith a Christian. The deeper I got into the quest for quality and the Texas Quality and Malcolm Baldrige Awards, the more I discovered that, for me, the quest was linked to many dimensions of my personal growth, including the spiritual dimension.

Telling you about the quest in terms of my faith is an integral part of my story. I do not mean to suggest in telling it this way that you have to be Christian or spiritual to go on the quest or to achieve quality in the conduct of your business or to win the Malcolm Baldrige or any state award.

I do suggest, however, that you need to be prepared to be profoundly affected by the quest. Taking the risk to expose your mind, heart, soul, and spirit to its processes may have surprising results.

For those men and women who conduct their businesses and their lives based on religious faith, I also suggest that you need not fear losing your faith in the process of the quest for quality. On the contrary, I have found that the processes involved in achieving quality act as bridges among people of various faiths and philosophies, and, as Abraham Lincoln once said, "touch … the better angels of our nature."

Timeline of Important Dates

1946: Texas Nameplate Company formed by Charles Steineger, Tom Hampton, and Roy Crownover.

1952: Dale Crownover born.

1959: TNC moves to Ervay Street after former building collapsed.

1960: Dale starts work in paint department.

1971: Dale graduates from high school. Attends University of Texas at Arlington.

1972: Dale buys farm in Italy.

1973: Dad buys out partner Tom Hampton, buys Allstate Nameplate.

1974: Plant Manager drowns. Dale quits school, becomes Assistant Plant Manager.

1975: Dale goes to night school at SMU, is President at Allstate, and Asst. Plant Manager at TNC.

1978: Dale starts in sales at TNC.

1979: David Voekel, Vice President, quits. Dale becomes Vice President.

1980: Dale closes down Allstate.

1983: Dale and Dad disagree.

1986: Jamesbury sues TNC.

1988: Dale marries Julie.

1989: Dale settles lawsuit, is named TNC President; son Ryan born.

1991: General Dynamics demands TNC begin SPC program.

1992: Sales Manager leaves TNC with customer information; son Dan born.

1993: TNC celebrates its first Zero-Defects Day.

1994: R. B. Ewing almost quits.

1995: R. B. Ewing and Ranga Kambhampaty die suddenly.

1996: TNC wins Texas Quality Award, celebrates 50th Anniversary, and receives ISO 9002 certification, one of the first nameplate companies in the U. S. to do so.

1997: Dale graduates from college. TNC wins Texas Association of Business and Chambers of Commerce Award, Arthur Andersen Best Practices Award, and receives a site visit for the Malcolm Baldrige Award.

1998: TNC competes again for the Malcolm Baldrige Award.

 # I Heard It
on the Radio

It takes about an hour for me to drive from our small farm in Italy, Texas, to the Ervay Street location of Texas Nameplate Company in South Dallas. I get a lot of thinking done about Texas Nameplate on these drives.

The company has been a part of my life for as long as I can remember. Mom and Dad started it before I was born, in 1946, just a year before my older brother, Doug, arrived on the scene. Over the years from the age of six, I worked in various positions at Texas Nameplate. Then, in 1989, the year after Julie and I married, Dad named me president of the company and my first son, Ryan, was born. It was a neat year.

As newly named president, I would often remember on these drives into work the history of our family's company and the loyalty Dad had built up with our employees and our customers, including General Dynamics (now Lockheed Martin).

So you can imagine the concern I felt driving in one morning when I was told of some bad news that I had to face. I wasn't sure what the bad news might be, but as a young businessman I was not all that worried because we knew our business better than anyone did.

And Texas Nameplate was fortunate to have trusted employees with years of service who could weather any storm. There was my uncle,

R. B. Ewing, Troy Knowlton, Jimmy Spurger, Ernest Burleson, Avon Holley, Sula Reilly, and Verdie Jones, just to name a few of the crew that Dad had assembled over the years. Bob Mantle was one of the people I had hired and he was working out fine.

But among the other employees, there could be a wage problem or maybe an allegation of discrimination. Unlikely in either case.

Or maybe it was just one of those typical business concerns. Was someone threatening our market share? Was sales growth turning downward? Maybe someone was complaining about some price quote not being made in a timely manner or maybe a delivery date being missed. Did we not do sufficient overruns to fill an order with acceptable quality?

Was one of our key employees quitting? Maybe someone had a health problem. That would be tough. I knew that one. I had back surgery myself in 1987.

Could it be a problem with our water quality? That was becoming a major concern, especially with the Environmental Protection Agency looking so closely at the nameplate industry for hazardous production waste.

I hoped it wasn't a problem with my brother Doug. He had recently been named president of Identification Plates. That was Mom's company. Our brotherly rivalry had always been manageable, though I wondered at times whether our competition was what was driving us both in an unhealthy way.

The more I thought about it as I was driving, the more I figured it was just another problem with shipping our orders. Counting orders shipped was the only way we had of knowing whether we were fulfilling our contracts.

If it was something else, I would have to face the unknown one more time. Given my hands-on education, I was always a bit fearful of what I didn't know. If it was something in that arena, I would have to go and hire some outside consultant and then justify the expense.

That's when I heard it on the radio. What I heard changed my life and my attitude toward the problem I was going in to work to face. I don't remember now who said it or really all that he had to say. I just remember that on that particular day, out of the blue came a voice that said that only about one third of one percent of family-owned businesses in America succeed to the third generation.

It hit me right between the eyes. As president of Texas Nameplate, I was the second generation. My children would be the third.

Whatever today's problem was, I thought to myself, I've got a bigger one. Dad and Mom had given my brother and me the opportunity to succeed. Would I be able to do the same for my children? Would Texas Nameplate still be around for my children?

When the odds against me and the company hit me, I almost froze. Maybe today's problem would be the reason why we wouldn't make it. On the other hand, since Julie and I wanted to support our family, I knew I wanted to beat the odds for sure.

Roy Crownover, Founder
Chairman of the Board

How Texas Nameplate Got Started

"... It was back in 1946. We were all over at Mr. Webb's house sitting on the porch one night watching Joe Lewis fight and the three of us [Charles Steineger, Tom Hampton, and Roy Crownover] decided to start Texas Nameplate. So in order to do this, our friend, who was a notary, just drew up an agreement, a partnership. Doc Edwards said he'd loan us $3,000, '$1,000 for each of you boys.' "

Roy's True Partner

"... Now Mr. Steineger was the bookkeeper. We were doing the making and he was doing the invoicing. When I first started, Mr. Steineger kept his first job at the engraving company, Tom Hampton kept his job, and in the afternoons they'd come by. They always had income. That's why I come back to the importance of my spouse [Bernyce Ewing Crownover] from the beginning."

Opportunity Is What You Make It

"... I never worked good in school. I went through the 10th grade. I took the non-college industrials. We had a machine shop and Mr. Neff was the teacher. He had a radio and he was gone. Everybody was in class on machines and guys were talking. They wanted to turn the radio on and I said, 'Turn it on.' And they said, 'Can't, he locked it up.' I said, 'No problem.'

I took the top drawer out and turned the radio on and put the drawer back. Then Mr. Neff came in and stopped the class and said, 'Who turned on the radio?' So I stood up and said, 'I did.' He said, 'I want you to apologize to the class.' I said, 'No sir, I will not. You better hear the whole story.' He said, 'You still got to apologize to the class.' 'No sir, I will not.' 'Then we're going to go down to the principal's office.' So we went down there and the principal said all he could do was expel me from school.

"I went home and told my mother the whole story. 'You'll cool off tomorrow,' she said. But I had a part-time job and went back to work. I never went back to school. I don't regret that. Looking at the pictures of Steineger, Hampton and me, if this partnership hadn't occurred like it did, I wouldn't have ended up with this wonderful opportunity."

WHAT ARE
THEY TALKING
ABOUT?

When I got to Texas Nameplate that morning, the only thing I had on my calendar was a meeting over at General Dynamics in Fort Worth. Of all the potential problems I had mulled over in my mind, it never dawned on me that my scheduled meeting might be the source of the problem. But Uncle R. B. warned me that's where I'd find out more about it.

During 1991, General Dynamics had started sending us letters saying they were going to mandate that we, along with all of their other suppliers, become certified under their Statistical Process Control (SPC) program.

Wouldn't you know. I remember throwing all of those letters in the trash can. We had no desire to ever get involved with SPC. The little bit I had heard about its techniques for measuring and monitoring business processes wouldn't work well at Texas Nameplate. The certification process was very difficult, expensive, and only the "big boys" had to do it.

As a result, we had repeatedly told General Dynamics we would not submit a procedural plan for implementation.

In response they continued to tell us they would cut off any and all suppliers who did not submit a plan for implementation of SPC.

After a year of threats to cut us off, here

I was going to their EDI (electronic data interchange) meeting, in full denial of what might be happening.

The meeting didn't take long. Texas Nameplate had been cut off. I felt like I had been driving a car trying to outrun a train to an intersection, but didn't win.

When the reality of this train finally hit me, it wasn't so much surprising as it was shocking. I knew what was happening, but even though it was staring me in the face, I still didn't believe it was happening.

General Dynamics was a big train, one of Texas Nameplate's major clients. Their action would greatly damage our bottom line. Dad would surely be worried about bankruptcy.

As I drove back to our office, I struggled with what this really meant. Was this going to be a major turning point in the life of the business I had only a couple of years ago become president of or simply the beginning of its death knell?

I found myself remembering some of the turning points in my own life, trying to compare them to what I was facing now.

The first one I remembered was when I was just a boy. My father bought me a riding lawn mower and I started mowing for some money. I had to pay him back one half of my income until I paid off my "equipment" loan.

I learned the value of money and how to take care of my equipment. What's more, I seemed to always have money when my buddies didn't. But I was also the one out working when they were playing.

Maybe General Dynamics was thinking they were providing us with a new "riding lawn mower" that was going to make us both more money. I didn't see it that way. I saw more hard work, a heavy expense, and a big "loan" of time to pay off. I didn't think we needed it.

Then I remembered another turning point. When I was 20 years old, I bought a farm that many probably said I didn't need. I really didn't have a lot of money, but my grandfather always said they will never be able to make any more land and that it would be a good investment.

Like with the lawn mower, I learned fast what it was like to watch my expenses and be involved with a budget. It was tough, very tough, for a while to make ends meet, but I really learned a lot.

Maybe what General Dynamics was doing was trying to make us go through a learning experience and virtually take over the "farm" that we had all worked on for so long.

My mind raced over other turning points in my past: when I left college in the midst of running for my fraternity presidency and, without graduating, went to work for Texas Nameplate; when I got married to Julie after waiting all those years for the "right" woman; and when we had our first son, Ryan.

It was as if General Dynamics was telling me I had to leave college again. It was as if they were telling me whom I had to marry, and what would be the fruit of that marriage. The pace of my thoughts kept rushing by just like the traffic outside my car until they both slowed down.

I had to admit, it wasn't like General Dynamics hadn't given us a choice. They had. We had been opting not to take them up on their offer.

It wasn't like General Dynamics hadn't allowed us time to make a judgment on the matter. We had. And so had they. It felt like we were being fired. It was not a good feeling. Friends don't fire friends. There was a sense of betrayal.

But as I drove on, it was clear that I was facing more than a turning point, more than a choice, and more than a judgment. I was being forced to make a decision.

Like most people, I had not made that many really big decisions in my life. The three I remembered involved me at the most personal of levels. Leaving college ahead of time and marrying Julie were not just choices or judgments, they were crucial decisions, like the decision when I accepted Christ as my Savior.

While I was born and raised a Baptist, I was able to make my own decision at my own time about being baptized and accepting Jesus. Like when I left college or married Julie, there was no pressure from anybody, just me admitting it was the right thing to do and the right time. When I accepted Christ, it was a big thrill for me because, even though I was around the Baptist theory all my life, I was excited that I waited until I really knew what this decision really meant.

When Julie and I married I had the same thrill. And I had the same sort of "right" feeling when I left college, though I still wanted to go back many times and finish.

You might say that General Dynamics was telling me to convert to their new form of religion. That's a hard thing to swallow for most people.

My core beliefs were formed early and I saw them practiced daily at Texas Nameplate. Uncle R. B. believed in quality and had been at it for nearly 20 years. And he was the best Baptist there will ever be. A deacon with the First Baptist Church in Dallas under Dr. Crisswell, he used to talk to me a lot about beliefs and how they played out in the workplace. He and my dad had taught us to hold on to four key beliefs: honesty, loyalty, respect for elders, and fairness.

With General Dynamics' cut-off order, it was as if they wanted to add this SPC thing as another set of beliefs on top of what we already had. Since I hadn't accepted it, I was going to be — no — I had been excommunicated.

By our separate actions, General Dynamics and Texas Nameplate had forced each other to decide a single issue:

**Will we change the way
we do business with each other
to achieve better quality?**

Since General Dynamics thought they had our decision, they must have thought we weren't going to change. With so much at stake, I realized that we better give them more than our silence. But what?

R. B. Ewing
Quality Control Manager

Dad always said, "You be good to these peo-ple," meaning the Texas Nameplate employees. Uncle R. B., a deeply Christian man, agreed.

R. B. was one of my spiritual fathers. He pointed out some key passages that helped me in my efforts to lead Texas Nameplate on its journey. Here are two of them.

This first passage helps me with the "master-servant (slave)" attitudes some managers and employees get out of joint with. It helps diffuse matters, especially among believers, but also among all men and women of good will.

From *Ephesians 6: 5–9*
"Slaves, obey your earthly masters with fear and trembling, in singleness of heart, as you obey Christ; not only while being watched, and in or-der to please them, but as slaves of Christ, do-ing the will of God from the heart. Render serv-ice with enthusiasm, as to the Lord and not to men and women, knowing that whatever good we do, we will receive the same again from the Lord, whether we are slaves or masters. And, masters, do the same to them. Stop threatening them, for you know that both of you have the same Master in heaven, and with him there is no partiality."

This second passage helps me remember how we can work best with each other.

From *Thessalonians 5:12-15*

"But we appeal to you, brothers and sisters, to respect those who labor among you, and have charge of you in the Lord and admonish you; esteem them very highly in love because of their work. Be at peace among yourselves. And we urge you, beloved, to admonish the idlers, encourage the faint hearted, help the weak, be patient with them all. See that none of you repays evil with evil, but always seek to do good to one another and to all."

 # No Way

A friend once asked me this question: "If you knew you were going to die in 12 months, what would you do?"

It was a sobering question. My answer was not that slow in coming, though. I would first ask my family and then my employees what they would like for me to do in preparation for my departure. I would try to comply with their desires. If I had much to say about it, I would make sure my family was secure financially and would maybe write some letters for my children to read at a later date.

Now I realized that the issue I was facing with General Dynamics had a similar feel to it. What was I going to write my children about my decision? I had to treat my decision with just as much seriousness and attention as if I had been given my death notice. But when I began to look at the problem from this viewpoint, I gradually came to recognize that the reasons I was willing to lose all General Dynamics' business were based largely on the history of Texas Nameplate, its family culture, and my evolving role in it.

As I sat down at my desk back at the office, I tried to find the words to explain why I thought there was no way Texas Nameplate could succeed with SPC.

Notes and Questions

I made notes to myself about our history, our culture and my roles in the company, and also began to write questions as they came to me.

I started off with a funny realization about how ironic life can be. Just as General Dynamics was cutting us off, I was recalling my first memory of Texas Nameplate when I was about six years old. The roof of our building at the old Main Street location had fallen in. I remembered how my dad was bringing home equipment to store in our garage.

On normal mornings when I was a kid, Dad would leave home around 7:00 a.m. I can still see him driving off in his old Ford Ranchero pickup truck as I waved to him through the big front window of our house.

Dad's office was now just across the hall. Could I be as resourceful now as he was when the roof fell in? Did I have it in me yet to approach him about the problem?

Because of the roof collapsing, Dad had to move the company to its present location on South Ervay. When they first moved in, it was on a weekend and Dad took me along. He put me in charge of cleaning all the oil off the floor. The building had been leased earlier to a trucking firm as their maintenance center. It had oil spills all over the main floor.

The employees who worked for my father were there that first weekend as well. I got paid one dollar for a full day of pushing a homemade squeegee from the front door all the way to the back door. As you might imagine, it was a big building to me at that time.

How did this current mess compare with the mess I was cleaning up then?

From that time until I was about 13 years old, I spent just about every Saturday with my father either at Texas Nameplate or at his farm. He and I would stop and eat breakfast at the "Pig Stand" on Cedar Crest down the street before going to work.

Would doing this SPC thing mean I couldn't be with my family on weekends?

While Dad worked, I would play with the dollies that they used to move nameplates. All the employees would play and talk with me. This is when I started liking the people at work. I also started to learn how they respected my father.

Would our employees resist the SPC thing? Would they lose whatever respect they had for me? Would they long for the good old days when Dad was in charge?

My father would always talk with them, was always nice to them, and had fun with them. My father was never lazy and could do just about anything that needed to be done in the business. He said he would never ask anybody to do something he could not do or would not try himself. I am this way today because of his example.

Was I being put into a position where I would be asking my employees to do something I could not or would not do myself?

When I was 16 and got my driver's license, I really thought I was cool. Maybe it was because I could get out and do my own thing. When I was a little boy of eight, my dad taught me how to drive an old jeep. I loved to drive it anywhere he would let me. So when I got my driver's license, I was nicknamed "Hotrod."

I could understand the joys of being licensed to drive, but were there any joys in being certified in SPC?

I worked every summer at Texas Nameplate except one. That summer I worked for Mom at Identification Plates, the other business my parents had. It was where my brother Doug went on Saturdays with Mom.

What would Mom think?

The first summer I had a full-time job at Texas Nameplate was after I received my driver's license. I worked in the camera department. I took home about $68 per week. Since I had to pay Dad $50 per week for my 1965 Ford Falcon, I only had $18 left. I would then go fill up my car with gas, which only took $2. I had enough money to buy my lunch the rest of the week. I paid for the car that first summer.

How much was this SPC thing going to cost?

I remember Dad saying at the dinner table that he was either going to buy out his partner, Tom Hampton, or Tom could buy Dad out. In the end, Dad did the buying and it cost him a bundle. I later learned that beforehand Dad went and talked with Troy Knowlton, Jimmy Spurger, Ernest Burleson, and a few others who still work for us today, to make sure they would stay.

One day when Dad and I were watering the orchard at his Waxahachie farm, he told me he had paid Tom off. He told me he wanted to pay him off earlier than he had to, because he wanted Texas Nameplate to be owned fully by the Crownovers. It was a proud moment for the family.

Was I losing it? Dad was so strong when it came to dealing with the others. Would he ever put up with the arrogance of General Dynamics? Then again, Dad could be hardheaded. Were we being that way with a stubbornness that knew no bounds?

In 1971 I graduated from high school. I had loved it, but I'd had a very difficult time making good grades. I had to study a lot more than my friends. By contrast, school seemed to come easily for my brother Doug. That bothered me. And though I do not ever remember him making fun of me, I know it had the understandable effect of emphasizing our differences.

This SPC thing would be a challenge intellectually. Was I up to it?

After I graduated from high school, I did not want to go to college. My brother, then a senior at Austin College in Sherman, Texas, and on the dean's list, made some comments about what might happen to me if I didn't. As you might guess, I only remember the critical thrust of his comments and not the particular warnings.

When we all went to my brother's college graduation, Dad said how proud he was to have a son graduate from college, since he had made it through only the tenth grade. Dad put a picture of Doug's graduation in his office at Texas Nameplate. That picture bothered me for over 25 years.

Finally my parents and I agreed that I would go to college. But I made a deal with them. I would try my best and at least make a "C" on my grades if they would promise not to open my transcripts when they were mailed home.

When I went to college at University of Texas at Arlington, I was scared to death. I did not like college at all. After three years, my grade point average was 2.35 out of 4.00, just a little bit better than my promise of a "C" average. I did okay in all my classes except my first year of accounting. I made my first, and last, "F" in that class.

I hated the word "failure" so much that I could hardly stand to hear anybody just say it out loud. With SPC, would they want us to keep an account of all our failures?

My parents would very seldom come out to see the progress I was making on my farm, even though I was only 18 miles from their farm. I had built my own fences, barns, carports, roads, and planted a lot of trees. My brother had been out to my farm maybe three or four times in all the time I had been there.

There was a sense of isolation about this. Why were we being picked on? We provided the goods ordered. Did we need to have General Dynamics come see our progress?

The farm reminded me a lot of what happened for me at Texas Nameplate. I had the opportunity to do something special. On the farm I had to work hard, but I never received any praise or encouragement. I had to do everything myself, which was fine. If I ever needed anything, I had to ask. Nobody gave me anything. Maybe this is where I learned about desire and determination.

What was in this SPC thing for me?

My goal on the farm was to have all my land and equipment paid for. I bought the largest portion of my land from an older man, John Harvey, down the street from me. He had 105 acres and wanted me to buy it very badly. He told me he liked that I took a lot of pride in my farm. He made me an offer I could not refuse. I believe to this day that he wanted me to have it no matter what. He was also the man that taught me to "buy all the farm equipment, the barns, and anything else you need on the farm *before* you ever get married." I honored his advice. When it came time, I bought my biggest tractor, plow, and barn five months before Julie and I got married.

Of all the times for this to happen. I had only recently married and was a new father. Why did this have to happen now?

During my summer months at Texas Nameplate, I worked at just about every job. People trained me in making nameplates. I had a lot of fun. People were nice to me. Dad was good to them even though he did not have much money. And he wasn't making much profit.

How was SPC going to affect profits?

I started working full time during the summer of 1974 after Jimmy Spurger's brother drowned accidentally. His name was Royal Spurger and he was the plant manager. He had a really bad temper and I remembered as a little boy how he used to yell a lot at the employees. After he drowned, I remember my father making a statement that he was going to "pretend" Royal was on vacation and let "time" determine what would happen as far as a replacement.

Did General Dynamics want to replace some of our existing, long-standing processes? I knew my business, didn't I?

During 1974-1978, I took some night courses at SMU and Eastfield College, still trying to finish my college degree. I also got my real estate license and sold real estate for about

five years to earn some extra money. I was
working three jobs plus taking care of the farm.

*I'd worked hard all my life. The last
thing I thought I needed was another job called
SPC. What would my new wife and new son
say?*

Running the business between the years
1979 and 1989 was the most difficult. I was
young and had a lot to learn. Our company did
not have any real guidance and it seemed like
Dad just kind of let it run itself. All the problems we had were really because we had no procedures in place and our employees took no
ownership. As I looked back, I was surprised
we stayed in business.

My father and I finally had our first major blow-up about business in 1983. I had just
gotten my pilot's license and had started thinking about where I was going in life. When I was
younger I had wanted to work as an air traffic
controller. When I started flying, I felt in control and did not have to question my ability. I
thought maybe I was pretty smart after all because flying an airplane was no easy task.

I finally had the guts to tell my father
that I wanted more control at Texas Nameplate
and that I felt I was not appreciated. I told him I
was tired of always having to prove myself to
him or just about anybody. I never threatened to
quit, but I did not go to work for about a week.
Then he started letting me do more stuff at work
without interfering.

Who was going to be in charge?

My dream for my life outside of work was, of course, to be happily married with some boys. Many of my friends were getting married, but I wanted to wait and make sure I knew what I was doing at Texas Nameplate as far as running the business. And I wanted to get my farm in solid financial position before I got married. So I waited till I was 35 years old before I married Julie.

How would this affect my dreams?

In 1986, the Jamesbury Company sued Texas Nameplate. My father did not want anything to do with the attorneys or the situation. I did it all. It was terrible. I got very little, if any, support from my father and mother, and none from my brother during three years of endless depositions, court hearings, etc. I found myself defending myself instead of Texas Nameplate. The plaintiff was literally trying to take our business away.

Would we have to consult our attorneys about the legality of General Dynamics cutting us off over SPC?

After we settled that lawsuit in 1989, we had to deal with about eight violations with the City of Dallas on our water discharge. We took two of them to trial and won both of them. As defendant I'll never forget during "voire dire" being described by the city prosecutor as a criminal who polluted "the water our kids brush their teeth with." For my part I felt like I was trying to prove to anybody who would listen that I was not as bad as people wanted to believe or think.

It was beginning to feel like the "system" had gotten us. Was it enslaving us?

During this time, one of our employees filed an EEOC complaint against us. I had just terminated her and she was very upset. She talked another employee into filing as well. Again, I did not remember getting much help. It was me against them. I won both cases.

Would I win this if I chose to fight General Dynamics?

After much of the legal stuff was over, things started leveling out a little and I was able to just run the business. It was during this time that we began remodeling the building inside. We also built a new warehouse out on the back parking lot. This was one thing I felt I was good at doing, mapping out stuff and having a vision.

Did I just not want to see the vision General Dynamics had been projecting for the last year?

No way. There was just no way this was going to work. My reluctance was supported on all fronts. I had just too many objections. I didn't have to wait to get all the answers to my questions.

Or did I?

Julian Ramirez
Art Department

Security
"In 1960, right before I was fixin' to graduate and wasn't really looking for a job, I needed to have money to date my high school sweetheart. I didn't think I'd get it. But I applied and got the job the same day. Married my high school sweetheart. Been with them both for over 38 years.

"People ask me if I get tired of going to the same place to work, but it's bought everything I've needed, like my house and cars. It's taken care of my family."

Change
"We used to do art on the drafting board with ruler and ink, rubber cement and exacto knives. I never could understand how a computer could do our work. It was a really big change for me, very stressful. Now I look at it and it saves so much time.

"The computer design process basically replaced the camera department. It cut days out of the process and keeps true to the project tolerances. We learned it by crash course, mostly by hands-on and only looked at the books occasionally.

"Dale's stressing quality didn't come as a surprise to me. I never could figure out why you

couldn't have quality. I've always done the best
I could. Maybe some people didn't think something was important. It used to be if you didn't
really know the answer, somebody would say,
'well it isn't that big a deal, we'll just make it
over if it's wrong.'

"But the customer wants it right and will only
pay for what's right. If they have a shipment to
meet, one part, one nameplate could represent a
lot of money to them if they can't ship their
product without that nameplate."

Value
"Nameplates have a lot of information on them,
maybe voltage or capabilities. The valve plates
we make have to have the right values on them
or they could hurt somebody."

QUALITY
IS FREE?

When I was about 16 years old, I was out dove hunting with some of my brother's friends. A shotgun jammed, and I was standing right by it when they "unjammed" it. The bullet came so close to my head that it knocked me out. I thought I was dead.

The bullet that General Dynamics had "unjammed" was beginning to make that same impression on me. I talked with Uncle R. B., and he suggested that I give them a call and see if we could talk. So I did.

I called up a good friend of mine who was in a pretty high position at General Dynamics. His name was Larry Cameron. I asked, "Larry, can I come to Fort Worth and talk with you about us being cut off by your purchasing department?" He said yes, and R. B. and I went to General Dynamics.

The meeting started out friendly enough. Larry had one of his SPC coordinators with him, a guy named Steve Barrett.

When it came my turn to express my concerns, I had my notes and questions fresh in my mind. For the most part they heard me out with their best poker faces on.

But it didn't end that way. This fellow Steve Barrett finally made some comment about Texas Nameplate not wanting to improve its quality by using systematic processes. He was wearing his big class ring from some Ivy

League school. If I had been more conscious of what was happening, I'd have recognized my envy of his obvious education. But instead, I took a proud stand. I let him have a piece of my Texas mind. I'd worked on the quality of our products for over 25 years. I told him in no uncertain terms how much I thought he didn't appreciate that.

Well, one thing led to another and we were, all four of us, almost ready to go to the mat over this SPC stuff.

After I got past my anger, I was really embarrassed over the whole incident. I was so upset by the encounter that I said some things I really shouldn't have, though I didn't apologize to Larry and Steve until a year or so later.

R. B. later described all of this as missing the mark.

It was like the time we transferred one of our inside salesmen to an outside sales position. I thought I had explained it to him well, but the next week he came in and was very concerned about whether we wanted him to work with us anymore.

Another time I was going to donate some money to my sons' Christian school. I told them about my idea, but they never did respond to my request. Here I thought I was doing a good deed, but they did not take it that way.

Maybe I expected too much from them, but it really disappointed me. They seemed so uninterested in what we were trying to do for them. We ended up adopting a local public school down the street from Texas Nameplate called City Park Elementary School.

In both of these instances, it really bothered me that I failed to explain it better. Maybe that's what Larry and Steve over at General Dynamics were feeling. We were not sure what they really wanted even though they thought they had explained it correctly. Maybe they felt that we were simply rejecting their "good deed". Maybe they figured they'd just "adopt" another nameplate company and move on.

I'm most at ease or most peaceful when I'm playing golf or working on the farm on the weekends. That's when I get some time alone with God. This was shaping up to be one of those times.

When I pray, I always pray that God will make the right decisions and that though He and I may not agree, that I will have the courage to accept His will for me. I also pray for the families of people who are sick. I don't usually pray for the dead since I figure God's taking care of them already.

This time I was "sick" about what was happening and I prayed. As I drove my tractor plowing up the field for a new planting, I asked God to help me see my path with General Dynamics.

My experience had been that God didn't always answer my prayers directly. So I was open to listening for His indirect answers, which came in any number of ways. I would usually begin my listening by talking with members of my family.

I loved family life. Based on the exam-

ple of my parents, Julie and I loved being together every night. We ate together, watched
TV together, and played with our children all
the time. When I was not able to be with my
family, I missed them. They were and always
will be my life.

My wife Julie talked with Mom everyday. They got along really well. I saw Dad at
work three days a week. Our relationship was
neat.

Dad's full name is Roy Douglas
Crownover, and Mom's is Bernyce Ewing
Crownover. Though getting on up there in age,
they still walked together every morning for
their exercise. They were very active. Dad still
raised cows and "messed" with his farm.

Mom worked with the Waxahachie
Chamber of Commerce in addition to running
her own Identification Plates business.

Mom and Dad had made indelible marks
on me in the way I lived and worked. They even
named my brother and me after Dad's first and
middle names. My brother is Richard Douglas
and I am Roy Dale. We are all "RDC's." Julie
and I would name our children the same way.

The difficulty I faced this time was that
my father was against the SPC thing.

Mom and Julie would only come to my
assistance if I asked them. I was determined to
handle this myself.

I'd learned from early on that I shouldn't
expect anything but maybe an "opportunity" to
do something. Even though my parents taught
me how to work and have respect for others,

they also encouraged me not to be lazy, do my best at whatever I did, and have fun.

Mom always used to tell me that it did not matter what I made on a test. What mattered was whether I tried my best.

That's what I wanted for my children. Julie and I wanted to prepare our children to go out into the world with respect for elders. We wanted them to listen more than talk and to do their very best at whatever they were trying to do.

I began to realize that we wanted our children to be able to look at the good side of everything, not just the worst. Things could always be worse than we thought, anyhow.

We would want them to learn how to get along with people, have fun and be happy. We would want them to learn how to accept things that God puts before them.

It was some time during these trying days after meeting with Larry Cameron and Steve Barrett that R. B. came into my office. He told me he wanted to tell me a joke. This was certainly unexpected. I was not in the mood and it was a bit out of character for R. B. to approach me this way. But I told him okay, it might ease my concerns.

He then asked me if I remembered the difference between my brother Doug, and myself. I told him I didn't find our differences that humorous. He reminded me that as children Doug would always go around asking "why?" and, by contrast, I would always respond "why not?" I agreed that's how we'd been since we were kids.

R. B. said this joke reminded him of Doug and me. He went on:

"There was a young father of twin sons. One an optimist and the other boy a pessimist. On their birthday, while the two boys were at school, the young father filled the room of the pessimist with toys.

"The optimist's room ... he filled his room ... with manure.

"When the boys got home from school, they immediately went to their respective rooms. The father later went upstairs to see them.

"The pessimist, with all his toys, was crying out loud. The father asked, 'Why are you crying? You have all these neat toys to play with.' The little boy said he was crying because he did not know where he was going to put them all. He said that he was concerned because his friends might become jealous. He also was upset because he was going to have to spend a lot of money on batteries for many of them to work.

"Finally, the father went down the hall to the optimist's room where he heard his other son laughing and singing out loud, shoveling through all the manure.

"The father asked him, 'Why are you so happy shoveling through all this manure?' The boy responded, 'Dad, with this much manure, there is bound to be a pony in here some-where!'"

R. B. didn't stick around to explain the

joke to me. We just laughed together as he walked out. He knew, as I was only becoming more and more aware, that my fate was not like my brother's. Our fates were different, though we each had our good days and our bad ones. I knew it was time for me to shovel some more manure and look for the pony. God had sent me His answer.

The first SPC procedure plan that R. B. and I turned in for approval by General Dynamics was three quarters of a page long. The one that finally got approved three months later was about 45 pages. There was a lot of manure before you got to the pony.

We used to laugh about that. R. B. always wanted Texas Nameplate to be the best nameplate company in the United States. He loved being the quality control manager. But I was the first at Texas Nameplate to take the SPC course on my personal computer from 30 lessons General Dynamics provided me on computer disks.

It wasn't easy, but I wasn't going to let it get me down. I approached it like a game.

When I was young, I went to a lot of Dallas Cowboys' football games and admired the way Coach Tom Landry handled himself. I thought it was neat that even if the Cowboys lost, he was always thinking positive. I adopted that approach to learning this SPC thing.

I also learned from Coach Landry's example that winning was not everything, despite what other famous coaches said.

Coach Landry always put God and family first and then football, in that order.

One time I had a chance to meet him in person. We were at a dinner. I was able to speak with him briefly about one of the football games where the Washington Redskins had just beaten the Cowboys. He was so cool about it. I think the loss bothered me more than him.

I also relied on Dad's example. He was always able to handle hard times. No matter how bad things were, he accepted the situation and did his best.

When I was going through these computer courses, R. B. brought me a book he had bought. It was entitled *Quality Is Free,* by Philip Crosby. He had read it and wanted me to read it too.

It inspired me to talk with R. B. about how great having "zero defects" in the workplace would be.

At first I joined him in laughing about how there would be no way our people could do that. But I was intrigued by the idea, so I went to talk with one of our managers, Troy Knowlton.

Troy was one of my first bosses at Texas Nameplate when I was just a kid. I admired how unbiased he was when it came to making tough decisions. He was always able to look at the big picture when it came to making big decisions. He was not for or against zero defects.

What I wanted to know from him was whether Crosby was right. Was quality free? Troy said he'd have to study it, but he knew that if the costs of doing SPC didn't outweigh the income generated by it, then you could say it was free.

The harder question, Troy said, was not whether it was free in the monetary sense, but whether it was free in all the dimensions that affected Texas Nameplate.

To discover that answer would take more than just Dale Crownover studying it and becoming certified in SPC. It would take several key players at Texas Nameplate to evaluate it. To have that kind of evaluation would cost money and time.

Thus I was learning that the journey to quality is like love. It is free, but it takes a lot of worthwhile work to discover its real value. Fortunately, I knew about love from my parents and especially from my wife Julie.

Julie Crownover
The "Right" Woman for Dale

"My sister Judy and I (we're identical twins) were waitresses at a little café in Italy, Texas. We worked there on Saturdays. Dale would come in every Saturday. We'd kind of fight over who'd wait on him. He was kind of exciting, somebody new, and we loved to talk to him. He wasn't the usual country boy. He was the hardest person in the world to wait on. When he didn't like what we had on the menu one day, he wanted to write his own menu. So we finally just said 'you write your own menu.'

"We kind of lost contact with Dale until a neighbor, who sold Dale his farm, passed away. I went to the funeral with my grandmother and I saw Dale there. He asked what we were doing after the service. He said he'd go over with us to the café. At the time I was in my third year at Baylor University and I was returning there that afternoon. He said he'd call me. Meanwhile, he started seeing my sister on occasion. So I kind of blew it off. Well, then Dale called me at Baylor and we went out to dinner. Since I was 21, people told Dale I was too young....So I put it on the back burner, but Dale and I would talk anyway. Eventually we became more serious and meanwhile Judy had met another fella.

"After dating for five years, Dale and I decided it was time to get married. But Dale is so 'plain Jane,' he wanted to have a small family wedding. Of course, I would have liked to have a 'real' wedding like my sister who had all the bridesmaids and the big reception. But I respected his point of view. He wanted a simple wedding at home by the pool with his family and Uncle R. B. Our pastor came to the house and there was an organist, but there wasn't anything fancy. Mom and Dad catered the dinner. Then in the middle of it all, an awful storm came up and interrupted everything for a while.

"Later we took our wedding pictures. If it weren't for Dale's idea of having our simple wedding outside, even knowing there might be a storm, we wouldn't have this beautiful picture from our wedding." (See page 206.)

SOME FIGHT, SOME FLEE, SOME SURRENDER

It was one thing for me to study SPC and begin to talk to others about getting involved. But once it became more apparent that I was intent on going forward with turning SPC into a reality at Texas Nameplate, the human consequences began to play out in at least three ways.

I was not adequately prepared for the consequences of stepping through the threshold that separates theory from practice. It might as well have been a wall.

I came to understand first hand that whenever change of a threatening sort is implemented from the top, some within the organization, like warriors on a battlefield, will fight it, openly or covertly. Some will flee it, taking their "justice" with them. And some will surrender, but not without dragging their heels. Only a few will embrace the change whole-heartedly, following the leader's vision.

The particular way this played out at Texas Nameplate undoubtedly had to do with the history of my evolving roles here.

When I first became the assistant to the production manager, my father and I did not speak much. He never really coached me or taught me much about running the business or how to make nameplates. I was to learn from others. And I did.

My father gave me the opportunity, but that was it. For reasons more obvious to me now than then, I was never really given much praise about any improvements I had made, or compliments about the job I was doing, or correction about the job I was not doing. Whether or not it was true, at the time I felt I had to prove to Dad, Mom, and even to my brother, that I was capable of being "somebody" at Texas Nameplate. I did not give much thought to the idea that they were trying to avoid being seen as favoring me simply because I was their son and brother.

This uneasy feeling inevitably bled into my personal life and into work at my farm, especially before I was married to Julie.

During this time, as might be expected, I grew up a lot and started really seeing myself as "maybe" being able to eventually run the company.

I went to work in the sales department in 1978. I traveled from time to time. I learned the importance of customer contacts and really knowing what our customers wanted from us.

In 1979, our vice president, David Voekel, told my father he was quitting after working with us for about 12 years. He was the son-in-law of Dad's former partner, Tom Hampton. David and I had gotten along well. When David left, I was named vice president.

I soon hired a good friend of mine from high school to help us out in the sales department. He worked for us for over a decade in sales. Then in 1989, Dad named me president.

With that brief history, fast forward to our implementation of SPC. Shortly after we began our SPC effort, I realized my old high school buddy and I could no longer communicate.

The challenge of SPC and our growing interest in quality control apparently had proven too much for him. Some fight, some flee, and some surrender to change. From my viewpoint, my friend had chosen to flee. He probably determined that his sales processes, whatever their quality level, were not going to be controlled by anyone other than himself. In February 1992, I asked him to leave.

He went to work for one of our major competitors. We heard from reliable sources that he provided them a copy of our price sheets, customer lists, and other proprietary information. His parting blow really bothered me since I also knew the person he went to work for.

I was determined to get our customers back, but in a different manner. Dad taught me a lot about ethics in the workplace. Even though I believed what was done was unethical, I was determined to be a step ahead of their way of doing business.

Over the years there were only a few moments when Dad and I were so near real despair. This was surely one of them. The hurtful way my friend chose to flee transformed him from a friend into ... well, not a friend anymore. There was not much we could do about the ethics of his choice. The old saying "what goes around, comes around" was only a small comfort under the circumstances. I took comfort, instead, in the birth of my second son Dan.

As one of the unintended consequences of this incident, I began to feel more pressure for choosing to go forward with the SPC certification from key members of our management team.

For about a year, Dad had been complaining at work that our prices were too low. When our customer lists were compromised in the midst of this change to SPC and quality processing, there was renewed interest in the company's financial situation.

Some senior people, loyal to my father, may have seen this new SPC effort as a waste of assets at a time when conservative fiscal practices like those championed over the years were needed. Because it was difficult to account at times for the cash value of the efforts we were undertaking, I suspected their opinions were most likely presented to Dad in various forms. These covert challenges to the authority of the company president went directly to the CEO, my father, who was not completely sold himself on SPC.

It wasn't that Dad would allow his son to be undermined. On numerous occasions he had made it clear to everyone that Texas Nameplate could only have one boss and that was the president, who happened to be his son. He had promised not to interfere. And he didn't.

Nevertheless, these challengers had chosen neither to flee the effort nor to surrender to it. Instead, they chose to fight it by effectively requiring that our quality programs prove themselves on a financial basis, in short order if possible. And while that was certainly a desirable result, the extra pressure was not. I watched as my long-term relationship with these folks became awkward, largely hidden, rivalries at best.

Finally, of those remaining who surrendered to the new process at their president's suggestion, the line drawn between those who did so willingly and those who did not appeared to split along the lines of tenure.

Those who had been with Texas Nameplate longer weren't as willing to change. Ernest "Goose" Burleson is one example of those senior employees who held back.

Those who had been here less time and who saw an opportunity to advance embraced it. Robert Hodge, Jr. is an example of those junior employees who didn't hold back.

Too much energy can be lost with such a divergence of directions. But General Dynamics did not promise it would be easy. They only promised we would not be cut off if we were certified.

The war for the future of Texas Nameplate had begun. And while it was certainly a civil war in every sense of that term, I quickly discovered that SPC certification was only the beginning of a longer struggle to transform Texas Nameplate into a company committed to quality.

Verdie Jones
Expedite Team Leader

Communicating Change

"I can remember when Texas Nameplate was just a big open place, and you froze in winter and burned up in summer. After Dale got into SPC and the quality journey, we really started growing. People started communicating with each other, working as teammates, not working harder but working smarter. It used to be that employees didn't have a chance to be involved, but now we keep each other up to date."

Where Giving Credit Leads

"When Dale speaks, he doesn't ever give himself the credit. He's always giving the credit to his employees. He lets everybody know this constantly. And that was a big change. People with common sense know it wasn't all him, but now he lets us know he knows he couldn't grow if we don't grow. I appreciate this. He's letting us know that we are the ones causing him to be where he is right now and that means a lot to us.

"Dale is a person that has really come a long, long way since the 60's when I came here as one of the first black women at Texas Nameplate. With my personality, you either like me or you don't. I've always been outspoken. Dale has shown me a lot … how a person can really change. He's growing too. He makes me feel like, 'you help me and I'm gonna help you.' I can say that Dale really has become a leader."

Soul in the Workplace

"... That's when Dale got into the Bible. We had always been talking about different passages. He showed me a book of his and was saying stuff about the Bible and I said, 'Man, I'd like to have a book like that.' And he bought me the book. And it cost some money. I still have it. That's the type of relationship I have with my boss. When you put God in your life and God over everything, God gets involved and Dale knows it. Like I tell him, it's not about not knowing the Word, but knowing the Word and not doing it that causes problems."

THE KITCHEN WAS HOT

Harry Truman once said, "If you can't stand the heat, get out of the kitchen." During Texas Nameplate's civil war days, some of our senior employees who weren't particularly interested in making changes were gradually turning up the heat. The kitchen was hot and I had to stand it.

Besides Ernest Burleson, those offering me a challenge included Troy Knowlton and Jimmy Spurger, even Uncle R. B. and Dad.

My approach to working with them was simple at first. I just kept throwing the SPC lessons at them and made them come to me to find out what it was all about, since I was taking the certification training first. This worked to a point. But it was like herding a bunch of cats.

What I thought I had to do was employ the skills of a teacher. What I learned was that I had to become a true educator. There is a difference. For example, if I ask, "What is your attitude towards the world?" you likely will have one opinion and someone else will have another. I can tell you what my opinion is too, like a lecturing teacher. I can tell you I am concerned about all the violence that is always going on in other parts of the world and about the continuing nuclear threat in the world.

So now we have several opinions about the world in general. That's like asking about general attitudes towards SPC. It would get me answers from everyone, but the answers were not moving us forward at all.

Let me throw out another example. Suppose I focused the question more sharply and less globally. I could ask, "What is your attitude towards our country?"

For myself, I really love being an American. When I was younger, I went to Europe and traveled through thirteen different countries and found out the hard way how nice it is to be from the United States. I have a hard time when anybody does anything disrespectful with our American flag or does not pay respect during the singing of our national anthem at sporting events.

Several problems arise though. The "world" of our employees is likely to be much more focused on their everyday life. Also, some of them are not from America. They may be trying for their American citizenship, but may not have obtained it thus far.

But I'm not just talking about nationality differences. SPC can be learned by all nationality groups. The problem is deeper. What if I asked, "Which figure in history do you most admire?"

Because of its prominence in America, I really admire the Office of the President. I enjoy learning about the internal operations of the White House and, because of my interest in flying, of Air Force One. I think our Presidents, the White House, and Air Force One symbolize the best in our country.

But while I know I would give almost anything to be able go inside Air Force One, many of our employees would never be that interested in such historically compelling people or symbols of government. They would more likely be interested in the times of their own lives than in those of other people, especially from another century.

Thus, any of my lessons about SPC that included information about the history of organizations most likely did not cut it. SPC had to be seen as relevant to our employees during their own time at work.

Now, anyone who knows me also knows that I can not stand lazy people. I also have a problem with people who are unorganized or who are not willing to try and go to another level. So my initial difficulty when trying to teach others about SPC was not being patient enough. I had to have patience, a lot of it.

I also learned about humility. While I really do feel that you make your life as good as you want it to be and that you have to want to be happy, not everyone shares such beliefs.

I am as proud of my accomplishments as the next guy, but when it came to teaching SPC, I had to learn about a fairly strange thing called paradox. I had to take pride in being humble. What seemed at first to be a contradiction turned out to be a source of new insight for me. Let me give an example of what I mean.

How would you tend to react to a flat tire on the expressway? If you're not in a big hurry, this may not be a big deal. But if you're trying to make a scheduled meeting, the pressure to get the tire changed can be enormous.

Changing flat tires really doesn't bother me. Don't forget, I live on a farm. Between flat tires and dead batteries, I've had my share of unexpected delays.

And while my main concern in such situations would usually involve the amount of air the spare has or whether I can recharge the battery, when I was working with our employees, I had to do the opposite sometimes of what I would have expected.

Though I knew I had a scheduled meeting with General Dynamics, it was almost as if I had to deflate myself intentionally to get our employees to roll forward and accept SPC. I had to remember that though I was working off a supercharged battery, they were not, at least at the beginning. I had to turn my energy level down to get theirs to go up.

Now some might think that this approach required as much knowledge of company politics as it did SPC. I can't deny that my company has its share of politics. But I'm not naturally given to thinking that way.

I think our employees gradually realized that not only did I mean business by my efforts, but that I was concerned about their futures as well as my own. I was not simply dictating a new policy. I was trying to let them discover it themselves.

Over a period of months, we were able to put into place the necessary measurements to fulfill the requirements for SPC certification.

However, like so many things, after the newness of it wore off, our processes started fading a little bit. This is really where I came up with the idea of taking it to the next level. I became concerned that we had done so well with the in-house training that maybe our people would retreat into their same old habits.

My next move was getting started with Total Quality Management or TQM. (See *Glossary*.) I felt we had to do something else to keep SPC going strong. So, following Uncle R. B.'s lead after reading the book he had given me, I went to Philip Crosby's "Quality School" in 1992. I went for five days and loved it.

After all was said and done, I was tempted at first to say it was really just a lot of common sense. But on reflection I had to admit that common sense is not evenly distributed. Some of the most significant ideas are often the hardest to achieve because they appear so simple. I had been through such a humbling process learning how to teach others about SPC that I knew I had only gotten my fair share of common sense, no more, but no less.

Though I liked the Crosby School, I was not going to rely solely on my own impression. I asked Bob Mantle, our sales manager, to go to the same class two weeks after I did. I wanted his educated opinion.

He liked it as well and thought it would work for Texas Nameplate.

Next we sent Jimmy Spurger, our plant manager, and David Norris, then our assistant quality control manager, to the same school.

When they returned, we all agreed that TQM would be good for Texas Nameplate. Bob, Jimmy, David and I started our first Quality Improvement Team. (See *Glossary*.) It was undoubtedly a major turning point of our civil war.

The kitchen was still hot, but there were more who could stand it.

We worked on TQM forever it seemed. We took advantage of our slow season and trained all our people at this time. We took the time for all the necessary internal team meetings that went into establishing a good foundation in TQM across the company.

After we got our TQM foundation laid, I again felt the need to take it to another level. I had heard about the Texas Quality Award. I wanted to apply for it because it was for the State of Texas, it was brand new, and I really thought we had some neat stuff.

We called for and received the award criteria. Then we started trying to answer the questions ourselves. It was a little bit more difficult than we had expected, so we hired a writer to help us.

He asked when the application was due. We responded that it was no real problem. We still had almost four weeks to complete it.

When we finally sent the application in to the Quality Texas Foundation, we thought without a doubt we would get a site visit and go on to win. More to learn. Not only did we not win, we did not even get a site visit.

We were devastated. I will never forget

how Bob Mantle and I went to Vincent's, a local Dallas seafood restaurant, to talk it over. We rode the roller coaster of our emotions over several whiskey sours.

We knew our Quality Improvement Team would agree never to apply again. We figured the award process was all political. The sting of defeat, if not the whiskey sours, was distorting our vision. Only later did we fully realize that we were simply not ready to win yet.

We acknowledged there was a silver lining in the clouds. During our efforts, we had made some important contacts with people like Warren Hogan and Glenn Bodinson of the Hogan Center for Performance Excellence, who knew how we could get better. They coached us to apply again for the award, if we were willing to learn and be serious players.

Then a funny thing happened, as it sometimes does in the late afternoon over drinks commiserating at lunch. We realized that when we had anticipated winning the Texas Quality Award, we had made reservations to attend the Malcolm Baldrige Quest for Excellence program in Washington, D.C. (See *Glossary.*) Now, given our defeat, we chose to cancel our trip to the Quest. Then we remembered something.

We had no insurance on the tickets. They were already paid for. So despite our disappointment and our decision not to ever apply again, Bob Mantle and I decided we might as well go to the Quest anyway.

Bob Mantle
Sales Manager

Embrace the Change
"I like it here. I like the change. There are no cut and fast rules here. You can come in, relax and do your job. It's not the same rut. Everyday there's something new happening. And you get to use your brain here and I think that's cool. We get to brainstorm new products and ask, 'why can't we do this?'"

Turn Around the Turnover
"You'd have to have been here 15 years ago to appreciate the change. When I started here, I came back in at 4:00 p.m. from selling and everyday I saw new faces. When we started the quality journey, it really changed. People are here to stay now. They take it like a home. Before, if you could fall in that back door, they'd hire you."

Work toward Bilingual Workforce
"We're doing Spanish training so all the managers will be bi-lingual. That's one of our goals. We also have an instructor teaching Spanish-speaking employees how to speak English."

Benchmark with Mystery Shoppers
"We have a Mystery Shopper Program where we actually buy the product. Let's say you're a manufacturer of nameplates. We'll give a lady this list of our competitors to call. We buy 500 of those products, shop their prices, and get

their products. Then we'll ask, 'did we get them in 15 days like you promised? How's your shipping, packaging, invoicing? Now, how are those parts?' We'll reject those parts and check out your customer service to see how you handle us. We benchmark everybody. I have samples of all of them under my desk."

Eliminate Chemical Waste?
"There are 2,239 nameplate companies in the U.S. Only 32 claim to do chemical etching like we do. A big reason they don't all do chemical etching is the environmental issues. What would it be like if we could not only minimize, but actually eliminate the chemical waste?"

Import the Quality Culture
"I think Dale's goal is to buy another established organization rather than start a new one. He'd import the quality culture in a heartbeat. I wouldn't want to see him do anything else."

THE DARK
BEFORE DAWN

So Bob Mantle and I went to the Quest. And even though we hadn't won the Texas Quality Award, we were determined to learn more about the Malcolm Baldrige National Quality Award. As we learned, the two awards are based almost completely on the same criteria.

In Washington, D.C. at the Quest, we learned much more than we expected. One small example suggests what I mean.

We were sitting in the lounge one night, after the presentations for the day, and this lady was sitting there next to us. We struck up a conversation with her. It turned out she wrote applications for the Baldrige Award.

We kept talking to her and I said, "I wish we had a good writer," obviously still hurting from our experience with our first writer on the Texas Quality Award application.

The lady said, "It's really not that hard."

I responded, "Well, we really have no way to get competitive data." One of the items we fell short on with the Texas Quality Award was this kind of data.

She snapped back, "Give me a break, mister! Don't you have a sister or a wife that could act like they wanted to buy something and get you other companies' prices?"

Of course, Bob and I almost fell off our barstools. We just couldn't imagine some stranger telling us that. So I said, "That's not very ethical." I was thinking about our compromised customer lists a few years earlier.

She asked, "Why not? How are you ever going to find out whether your prices are any good if you don't do it?"

There were many encounters like this one on our Quest trip. Bob and I realized that we were beginning yet another learning curve. Because of our conversation with that lady, we later started our "Mystery Shopper" program that Bob loves to tell about, now that we have it up and running in what we believe to be an ethical manner.

We learned many other things at the Malcolm Baldrige Quest and met many others who were applying for the award too.

We were so taken with what we learned that we knew we would be exploring even deeper mysteries with the Baldrige than we had in our pursuit of the Texas Quality Award. What lay in store for us? We were not completely sure. But we did know three things.

First, we were going to celebrate our successes better. We had succeeded in applying, for example. We weren't going to waste time worrying about not winning, when so many others didn't even go up to bat.

Second, we were going to apply again and win the Texas Quality Award the next time. We were going to take all of the critical feedback and work on it so we would be better the next time we faced the pitcher.

And third, we were definitely undertaking the Quest for the Malcolm Baldrige Award, big time.

But to do this, I knew that I had to really clear the decks, although not in the areas you might expect. I had to do some powerful soul-searching to understand what I was doing and why I was calling on my company to go this route.

So on the plane coming back from Washington, I began to anticipate that I was going to be operating in the dark for a while before the dawn arrived. I knew what that meant on my farm. I'd gotten up many mornings before the sun rose, not knowing what the day was going to bring, but looking forward to it anyway.

By the time we got back to Dallas, I knew it was time for me to take a personal inventory so I could approach this Quest with all my heart, mind, soul, and spirit.

I wanted to learn more about why I was doing all this in the first place ... not just for my family and for the company. I had to know what was in it for me.

This part of the journey proved more difficult than I expected. I was not naturally self-reflective ... never have been. I knew I was just as dedicated and committed as the next guy, but I was never as self-absorbed as many others often seemed. Now I realized I had to know myself well first if I was going to lead my company on this Quest.

So I began my personal inventory from the outside and worked my way inward. This approach proved helpful to my thinking about how Texas Nameplate Company was perceived by others.

Looking at myself in the mirror was hard to do at first, but it's what I had to work with and it was as good a place to start as any.

If someone were to ask me what I liked best and least about my physical appearance, I'd start by answering that I was fortunate not to be overweight and laugh about not yet having that big of a nose.

Texas Nameplate, likewise, was fortunate not to be on the "overweight" side of things. We had only a few buildings on two modest sites. Given our commitment to safety and environmental concerns, we didn't have a "big nose" problem either.

Looking in the mirror I had to face it that lately I'd begun to develop some big bags under my eyes. It was more than just the long work hours. The signs of age and the stress of looking for insights sometimes have a way of showing up where you least expect them.

Likewise, at Texas Nameplate, there were signs of our company's age and efforts over the years to improve on what we had. It was not an unexpected look, especially given where the buildings were located. What my eyes needed was some rest. What our buildings needed was a fresh coat of paint.

For myself, my full height didn't arrive when I planned for it. When I was 16 years old and got my driver's license, I was only 4'10" tall. The police stopped me thirteen times because they thought I was too young to be driving. The real reason, I'm sure, was that they could barely see me behind the wheel. I'd always been a late bloomer, though, so my six-foot height had to wait and come later.

Likewise, for Texas Nameplate to compete for the Texas Quality Award and then the Malcolm Baldrige Award, we would have to remodel the attic of the main building to gain the space and height advantage we needed to see what was ahead of us. We hadn't needed it before, or at least we didn't think so.

Since as far back as I can remember, I've dressed conservatively. Julie calls it "plain Jane" conservative. I like short hair, white shirts, dark pants, and a normal tie. I just try to look like a Coach Tom Landry type businessperson without the hat.

Texas Nameplate reflected this business-like, traditional look inside and out.

I suppose if you haven't heard me speak, you'd only be guessing that I have a rather strong East Texas country accent. I do. But by now, you can also probably tell that I love using examples that compare work and home. That's East Texas, too.

Texas Nameplate was clearly established with East Texas voices, but our people now spoke with diverse voices and several languages. This was important to note in my inventory process.

When it came to personal habits, I began thinking that I was fairly free of vices, like smoking for instance. I think the reason I do not smoke is because my parents were big cigarette smokers when I was small, and I hated it.

But when I thought about that one example, I realized something else about the approach I was taking in my soul-searching.

Texas Nameplate, as with any group of people, has its own culture and its own set of "vices." And just as much as I hated the smoke when I was a child, I now had to look at the "smoke" we had all been giving off, including me. Whatever it was, we had all been inhaling it for years.

And, while I viewed our quest for quality as a breath of fresh air, I realized that some, including me, had preferred the older and, in my view, staler air of the past for a long time. Why? What was it?

When I looked at what was happening in this light, I began to ask deeper, less superficial questions about the company and myself.

What I knew about cigarettes helped me here. We all know now that they are addictive and potentially deadly. Sure, one cigarette most likely wouldn't kill you. But a steady, daily dose of smoke over the years will.

Could this simple insight help our company and me? I was onto something now.

When I had my back surgery, I learned fast the importance of doing daily exercises to regain my strength and flexibility. I figured that if I could discover the reason for my "smoke" and the company's, I'd be close to the answer that would give us all greater strength and flexibility.

Since it's usually true that where there's

smoke, there's fire, I aimed to find the fire. I reasoned that the closer I got to the fire, the closer I'd get to knowing what was in this quality journey for me. The answer was in the fire.

Looking for a "fire" in oneself or in a company is not that straightforward at first. It's not exactly like diagnosing a serious illness, such as cancer. I do not think I would deal with that too well, personally or in a company. Not that I would be selfish and afraid to die, but I feel as though I would be letting a lot of people down if I didn't try to fight it.

Moreover, based on what I knew of Texas Nameplate and myself, if we were being challenged at this point, it wasn't like a physical disease that could be cured with the typical "medication" of new employees' blood or the "surgery" of firing people.

Nor was it a matter of simply dealing with fears and prejudices. My worst personal fear had always been getting hurt in an automobile accident. I always do what I can to avoid car accidents.

For a similar reason, I had helped Texas Nameplate avoid the General Dynamics "accident" by instituting the Statistical Process Control program.

Given my white, male, middle class, Baptist background, I knew I had understandable prejudices that had tripped me up in the past. I had learned to overcome them, most likely the way most people do, I think.

I had allowed myself to get to know people like our employees Verdie Jones and

Kenny Howard. I learned that while I might not ever have the opportunity to choose their individual paths in life, they had the freedom to do so and the strength of conviction to follow their own lights.

Moreover, as I've gotten to know them, I have discovered that they are really neat people and just as capable as I am, if not more, of loving their loved ones and leading lives I appreciate more and more as we keep working together.

I learned early on that the environment and the people I associated with were very important to me. From my perspective, you are who you hang out with. I don't want to be in any environment I do not feel comfortable with. So looking for the "fire" down that path was not likely to yield new insights.

For a while I considered that the "fire" I was looking for was some form of unexpressed anger. I had always hoped that people would perceive me as being honest, respectful, and considerate of others. I knew that I usually handled anger pretty well. I am calm, do not raise my voice, and really try to think about what I am saying. I remind myself that the problem, whatever it really is, could always be worse.

Funny thing about this kind of self-reflection: the more I worked on what the "fire" was, the more I realized I was not getting mad or angry about it, but I was getting more determined to solve it. It was like a puzzle to me.

I have always been more of a thinker than a person who directs others, relates to them, or even socializes with them. I even have trouble at family reunions, despite my love of family. We all seem to be different in how we figure things out.

I have discovered that I must analyze matters before I make a decision. Others may be idealistic in their approaches, may look for ways to merge differing points of view, may be simply pragmatic or realistic. But I have to get to the bottom of things first.

So as you might expect, it took me a while to analyze all the factors that went into the "fire" that was causing the "smoke" in me and in Texas Nameplate.

Then, after a lot of hard work, it came to me.

I had been thinking about my heroes and what advice they would offer. My top four heroes had long been Coach Tom Landry, Roger Staubach, my grandfather and Dad. The problem of course was that, except for Dad, these men were not readily available for me to talk with. I found the critical clue from my thoughts about them nonetheless.

One of my fantasies was that I would wake up one morning as somebody unique like Coach Landry or Roger Staubach after going to bed the night before as just an anybody.

While I sometimes would imagine what it would be like to be chauffeured by limousine from my farm in Italy to the office, like I supposed they would be to theirs, I realized that was wishful thinking on my part. What was important was my burning desire to be a "unique somebody" and not just an "anybody."

In that one fantasy, I had identified my fire. As I analyzed it further, I realized that this fire fit into the pattern of my life and the role of Texas Nameplate in industry. I had relied on the strengths of others for years, in part because I was not sure of my own. At Texas Nameplate, we had built a business around the concept of making customized nameplates for other companies.

Then I remembered when I was a child having the most vivid nightmare over and over again. Somebody was in my closet and I would wake up scared and shouting for my parents.

Since I was unable to deal with whoever was in the closet when I was a child, naturally I relied on the strengths of my parents. I now realized that there was a part of me and Texas Nameplate that had been closed off for some reason and that my response and the company's was a form of fear.

When I got this far, part of the answer became clear. Whatever it was that I feared about myself and that Texas Nameplate feared would have to be led out of me and us through some process other than my own efforts. Somehow I knew I must give the "person in the closet" a better response than just fear. I didn't know how, but I knew I must.

If I was going to put us in the competition for the Malcolm Baldrige Award, I needed to get down to the bottom of that fear and face it. The sooner, the better.

Bernyce Crownover
On Dale and Doug Crownover

"Growing up, it was always the four of us. When the boys were younger, it seemed like Doug was always picking on Dale. One Sunday before church, the boys didn't show up. I asked what happened. Apparently Dale had had enough. He'd picked up a stick and hit Doug in the head. After that they always got along, though they knew better how to keep safe distance at times.

"Dale felt he was in Doug's shadow throughout school. But I told him, 'You are your own person. You don't have to worry about Doug.' In many ways, they were so completely different that at times I thought the only thing those two boys had in common was their mom and dad.

"Doug married the same May that Dale graduated from high school. Doug took a year of law at SMU and worked summers and weekends at my company, Identification Plates. Then he decided to come into the business. And I said, 'Fine, I'm tired of pushing.' And I retired. Everything went along real well.

"Meanwhile, over at Texas Nameplate, they were struggling for many years. But at ID Plates we never did have bad times. I had a real good string on it, knew everything that was going on, front and back. I had two supervisors work for me when men didn't work for women.

"About the time Doug took over my business, Dad named Dale president of Texas Nameplate. But while Dale was going through that Jamesbury lawsuit, Doug was still enjoying life over at his business. When Dale started this quality journey, the tables turned and things started going the other way at Doug's business.

"The boys took on different businesses by choice. They have respect for each other. They just want to do it their own way. It's difficult for Mom and Dad at times when Doug and Dale don't see eye to eye. We've never forced them to work their differences out. They have to find their own way.

"Dale has always had a wonderful, outgoing personality, whereas Doug was a more studious type. Dale was always listening. He'd go into town and listen to the old farmers. He retains more now than when he was young."

 Z-D Day

Perhaps you recall the story in the Bible of Jesus passing a blind man as he was walking along the road with his disciples. One of the disciples asked Jesus whose sin caused the man to be born blind, the man's or his parents'?

Many of us do not think in terms of "sin" anymore, especially in the workplace. We call defects in parts "nonconformances," meaning they do not meet project specifications.

Sometimes customers wonder how businesses can be so "blind" and cause such "defects" or "nonconformances." Some blame employees, like they blamed the blind man in the Bible. Others blame management, like they blamed the parents in the Bible.

As we went forward on our quality journey, we learned to take off our own blinders. Jesus answered his disciples that God's works manifest themselves even in what others see as defects. By changing our perspective on defects and nonconformances, we made a discovery that was nearly miraculous.

You see, for years my biggest regret was not having completed my formal education. Like Dad, I'm terrible in English. To this day, I can not spell and I have a poor vocabulary. As you might expect, over the years I developed a fear of writing. This did not bode well for someone who had chosen to submit written applications for the Texas Quality Award and the Malcolm Baldrige Award on behalf of Texas Nameplate.

As much as I may have wanted to express myself in writing in the past, I would never have attempted those applications, nor this book for that matter, without the help of others, so great was my fear.

I had always wanted to be smarter, book-wise. I freely admitted to envying some people who were really smart individuals. I believed my lack of more formal education was an obstacle to obtaining some of my goals. As a result I was less than confident sometimes in my own abilities. As for Texas Nameplate, it wasn't that different. No one working for the company had a college degree and many had not finished high school.

Yet, I realized I had useful strengths. I seemed to have more than my share of desire, determination, and commitment to get things done. A few at Texas Nameplate shared these strengths.

But I also had to admit to myself that I dealt with some people who had less than their share of these qualities. I did not always treat them in a tolerant way. When I finally had had enough of such people showing off or acting bigger than they really were, I even wanted never to forgive them, despite the fact that generally I have a warm heart for people.

Not surprisingly, the culture at Texas Nameplate was similar. What concerned me was that some at Texas Nameplate would see our effort to win the Texas Quality Award or the Malcolm Baldrige Award as a form of showing off or acting bigger than we really were.

But since I learned from my grandfather to be a man of my word, I basically wrote off those men and women who weren't trustworthy. They were like an old song that I didn't want to hear anymore.

For this quest for quality to be meaningful to me, I realized that it must help me discover the "music" that was locked up inside our employees and me. The music I'm talking about is the natural, genuine enthusiasm that people show when they like doing whatever they're doing.

The challenge for me was being able to listen to and watch our people play their new roles in our quest for quality and try to tell if they were faking it. As we continued the meetings and kept involving everyone in the quest, over time I could sense which people were only acting their roles and which weren't doing so well with it, mainly by their "music."

But you know, I quickly discovered that just as much as I was watching everyone else to try to gauge where they were with all of this, what was really happening was that everyone else was watching to see if I had the staying power to keep up this quest. They were looking to me to see if I really meant what I was saying, whether I really walked the walk or just talked the talk.

I don't remember exactly when I realized this, but it was a turning point in what others might call my leadership style. Let me try to describe the change.

When I was a young boy, my favorite TV show was called "The Beverly Hillbillies." Later, it was "Dallas."

Now, I'm not saying that my leadership style changed from that of a country bumpkin to a ruthless rancher. On the contrary, I probably had to change in the opposite direction.

I had to move back to my more natural roots of leadership to help others on our journey. I could not effectively lead Texas Nameplate by being a "J. R." to our employees. What I now found myself doing was more like what "Uncle Jed" used to do.

I would listen to what was happening in the minds and hearts of our employees, including upper management, and then act from what I was learning was my mission.

Being on a mission, though, is a tricky thing. When Jesus commissioned his disciples, he told them he was sending them forth as sheep among wolves. He urged them to be as wise as serpents and as innocent as doves. I had to act this way while we discovered what our real mission was. Learning to walk that kind of talk is like learning how to walk a tightrope without a net.

As you can probably guess by now, I did not start reading a lot of books until the last five years or so. It's always a humbling experience to admit it. But I do so openly, in the hope that my children and others who read this book will learn that they will be better served if they start reading earlier. Books are like a safety net. They tell you about what happened when those who went before you fell. I like books that are true stories, written by people who have experienced what they write about.

Most of the books I read were business management books. My favorite book at this time was *Quality Is Free* by Philip Crosby. I liked it because it was the book that best motivated me to take the quality challenge and commit to zero defects as a philosophy of doing business.

Although I have never really invented or created anything in my life other than building my farm from a very young age, I came to recognize that I had to be creative in my approach to bringing the quest for quality to Texas Nameplate. Our quest took a creative approach, given the type of culture and people we are. That's where I found my leadership skills mature.

Books, even this one, can only take you so far. The best ones speak in general terms and give solutions that usually work, but not always. Though Crosby's book motivated me, I had to figure out how to motivate my company.

Thus, my story here is only a snapshot of what really happens when you're in the actual situation.

For example, my favorite family picture is the one taken when Julie and I were married at our house. (You can see it on page 206.) Given where we were posed, it reminds me of one of the plantation scenes from "Gone With

The Wind." The photographer, Jack Odiorne, had it on display at his studio for a long time.

What it really captures for me is how and why I am so blessed. I had found the right lady for me and the right mom for my future children. The joy in my face over my beautiful bride still speaks to my heart whenever I see it.

Any book, even this one, aims at depicting the same thing for the story being told.

As Julie tells the story behind our wedding picture, you'd never really know, just by looking at it, the kind of stormy weather we had to go through that day. Though there are clouds in the background, you'd have to be told of the wind and rain that interrupted our ceremony.

When I think back about our first Z-D Day, the same thing must be said. What follows is just a snapshot of what occurred.

After working for decades to overcome the problems associated with defects and non-conformances in our products, on June 1, 1993, we publicly declared our first Z-D Day. It was like announcing your love for a woman on your wedding day.

We had a big luncheon to celebrate that Texas Nameplate was "wedding" zero defects to our company philosophy.

We had invited a lot of our customers and suppliers to the reception. Our banquet and the reception were a major success. Everyone present knew we had accomplished something big. It was the day on which I believe our quest for quality really began to pull all of our employees together. By that day, everyone at Texas

Nameplate had agreed, at least in principle, to make a commitment to making our products with zero defects.

This change in direction, mind-set, and level of commitment was essential.

No one describes all of this better than one of our most important employees, Ernest "Goose" Burleson. I invite you to read his keynote speech, which follows. But remember, like the wedding picture, you'll have to read between the lines.

If you do, you'll get a glimpse of the stormy weather we all went through before we got to Z-D Day.

"Pop's Speech"

When Ernest "Goose" Burleson, Texas Name-plate's self-taught, professional tool and die maker of the last 41 years, gave the keynote speech at the first Z-D Day celebration, his son typed "Pop's Speech." These are excerpts:

"I came to work for Texas Nameplate in February of '57. Many of you couldn't imagine the changes I've seen over the years. Each department would probably seem primitive by today's standards. Here are some examples:

"(1) The Art Department set lead type with little letters and numbers ... Cut them up and pasted them to artwork.

"(2) The Camera Department made hand 'step-offs' and developed them in trays.

"(3) The Printing Department mostly rolled ink by hand.

"(4) The Silk Screen Department...There was none until the late 60's and then for several years it was decorative only.

"(5) The Etch Department used powder and burned on open fire and vat etching.

"(6) In the Paint Department, there was no stripper. We baked with lights and hand-sanded.

"(7) In the Press Department we had a couple of foot shears, a couple of small and a couple of large presses. We had dies for ovals and some circles and the rest were cut on small presses.

"(8) In the Shipping Department we visually checked and picked the best to fill the order.

"As you can see, virtually every phase of producing nameplates has greatly changed for the better.

"Probably the most significant change at Texas Nameplate was when Roy Crownover bought out his former partner, became CEO and changed the direction of management for the better.

"Before that time Texas Nameplate operated so closely financially that sometimes you would have to try two or three places to cash your pay check. But, as you can see, this company now has the well-deserved respect and trust of its employees and the community.

"The next most significant change was probably when General Dynamics more or less forced Dale to initiate the SPC program.

"He became, or at least appeared to be, very enthusiastic about this program. I was very skeptical but fortunately I was in a position to lay back and observe.

"I saw SPC form more of a bond between department supervisors and give each of them more self-confidence and allegiance to Dale and Texas Nameplate. I took the SPC course and learned to 'talk the talk' and more or less go along but I was still very skeptical of this really solving many problems.

"In late spring of '92, Dale initiated our Quality Improvement Process after attending Phil Crosby's Quality College. This program really makes a lot of sense after understanding that zero defects doesn't mean 'absolutely perfect.'

"It had a lot of good common sense, with techniques and processes to help improve attitudes and performance. This was done through an education program taken in groups of ten for ten lessons. I've seen people with very poor work ethics kind of catch on and become outstanding employees.

"Just about everyone in the company has developed an understanding of work process models, flow charts, goal setting, and corrective actions. This has created more of an attitude of considering and changing the process instead of pointing the finger at the other guy.

"Through this improvement, we have met goals set for on-time delivery and rejection reduction for each period except one.

"I felt more or less forced to accept these

changes to begin with — and it certainly isn't easy to accept change at my age and tenure! Yet I sincerely believe these changes have greatly improved my attitude and ability in nearly all phases of my life.

"I'd like to sum up my observation on changes:

"To a younger person, change usually seems positive, as it tends to create new needs that he might fill as easily as a more experienced person.

"To an older person, change often will seem negative, as it tends to dislodge and uproot them from their comfort zone and the advantage of knowing existing systems.

"To a really wise person, change should be evaluated on an individual basis and considered positive with possible negative ripple effects that might outweigh the positives.

"I have worked through the excitement of youth, the challenges of being older, and hopefully I'm settling into the wisdom of accepting changes gracefully.

"I would like to thank Dale, Roy, and the rest of the management team for the patience and understanding they have shown in allowing me time to adapt to this program, which has proven you can 'teach an old dog new tricks.'

"If some of you are considering this program for your operation, I sincerely hope you can have this consideration for your 'Old Timers' while not stifling your 'Young Lions'."

 # EAST MEETS WEST

After Z-D Day, there was a sort of honeymoon period at Texas Nameplate. Lingering good feelings were shared by all.

Then, as you might expect, the day-to-day workload gradually edged out the memories of the "wedding" day and the honeymoon period came to an unremarkable end.

For my part, I was so uplifted by the success of our first Z-D Day, I immediately went to work on ways to solidify the gains we had made with our customers, suppliers, and employees.

What we needed was something that could help us put this new philosophy into actual practice and not just talk about it. What we wanted was a way to make this new marriage work so we could compete for the Texas Quality and Malcolm Baldrige Awards. To go forward with these two, sometimes divergent, routes on our quest for quality seemed almost impossible.

But no one could have predicted what happened next when our West met the stranger from the East.

As I've mentioned, Uncle R. B. was the Quality Manager for Texas Nameplate. He had been in this position for over two decades. Like everyone at the company, I had the deepest respect for him on many levels.

So you can appreciate how surprised I was when he reacted the way he did to the two proposals we came up with to satisfy both what we needed and wanted.

To meet our need, I proposed Texas Nameplate's first real guarantee for our customers. This would force us to practice what we were preaching. After many drafts, we finally put the Texas Nameplate guarantee like this: "Defect Free and On Time or It's Free."

With the success of Z-D Day, I thought the civil war inside the company was over. But adopting a guarantee this bold was almost too much for R. B. to swallow. Since he was in charge of quality management, he probably thought the task of enforcing the guarantee was going to rest on his shoulders. So he threatened to quit. Once again, I had missed the mark in explaining something.

Our quest for quality was finally beginning to hit home, closer than I had anticipated. Needless to say, it was a difficult time for me. In effect I was being put to the test and to a choice by the man who was the only true quality manager I had ever known. And he was my mom's brother to boot.

My uncle's threat to quit made me feel like I was being called out into the main street of some old town in the West. What was I supposed to do? Draw my gun on one of the men I loved most in my life or let him shoot me?

Then, almost like in some old Western movie, something none of us expected happened. A stranger rode into town and came to

Texas Nameplate. His name was Ranga Kamb-hampaty. He was from India.

To find help with writing our applications, we had placed an ad in the newspaper. Ranga answered it. He had run several businesses in India and lately in the United States. He had moved to Dallas to be close to his own family who had moved here to work for EDS in Plano, Texas.

After we described to Ranga what we were trying to do with the applications and the examiners' feedback we had gotten from our previous attempt, he at first did not want to apply for the state award. He wanted to "go for the gold," as he said, and apply for the Baldrige.

But Bob Mantle and I told him we did not want to go for the Baldrige just yet. We wanted to try and win the state award first. We told him we would be hiring him to help us with the Texas Quality Award. Ranga was willing to accept that goal.

At this point, I was ready to talk with Dad about hiring Ranga. But I was not completely prepared for his reaction. My father got really upset with me when I asked him. He said we did not need Ranga.

I told my father that I was concerned about the future of Texas Nameplate and that I really did not have anybody to help me "take it to the next level."

There is little doubt in my mind that Uncle R. B. was in part the unspoken subject of this conversation. He was obviously in the back of our minds. Our emotions were quite intense.

It was a bad meeting. But it worked out okay in the end and Dad let me have my way.

To compete for the Texas Quality and Malcolm Baldrige awards, I hired Ranga as our quality consultant to write the applications. This meant, of course, that Ranga would have to work with my uncle.

When Ranga met R. B., it was East meets West. And we all changed as a result.

In a very short time, I came to really admire Ranga. But, though I saw him as a God-send, he was not an angel. About Ranga there was good news and bad news to report … and then more bad news and good news.

As for the first good news, he helped our business in just about all phases. He taught us how to look into the future like through a kaleidoscope. He showed us how to plan strategically, create plan work sheets, and write out production processes. In short, he taught us a lot more than how to write an award application.

As for the first bad news, a lot of people at Texas Nameplate did not like Ranga. His assertiveness at times seemed to border on tyranny. His intellectual arrogance could at times be as foreign as his accent. That didn't sit well with some of us. He was very strong-willed and firmly determined to get us to change our ways of doing business, like we had said we wanted and needed to do. At times it was like he was rubbing our noses in it, though.

He pushed all of us very hard, to the point where some, including Troy Knowlton and Jimmy Spurger, were wondering if he was trying to take over Texas Nameplate.

At one point I remember Ranga telling Uncle R. B. that he wasn't looking healthy and that maybe he should get some rest. While that may have been a true observation, under the circumstances it did not play well. Bob Mantle and I knew what R. B. might have been feeling.

Bob and I had become really stressed out for two obvious reasons. First, we had let Ranga become almost too domineering. And second, we could not forget that he had been our choice despite my father's misgivings. We were struggling to handle our feelings.

There were others at the company, though, who loved Ranga's ways, his help, even Ranga himself. We did not always know which of us were in this group, but we found out on the day that we got more bad news about him.

He had died unexpectedly in his sleep the night before. He had worked with us only eight months and changed us all forever.

I will never forget how compassionate Dad was when we heard the news of Ranga's death. Not only was Ranga going to be missed during the final application process, but he had recommended that I reorganize a particular department and now he would not be there to back me up when the reorganization went down.

Dad listened and then encouraged me to go ahead with the plans Ranga and I had developed. Ranga had made the right recommendation. Now I had to learn to act on my own decisions and learn to live with them the rest of my life.

The depth of Dad's wisdom did not hit me right away. I was barely over the emotional shock of Ranga's death when it did. You see, Uncle R. B. died by the end of that same month.

It was at that point that I knew that for Texas Nameplate to face the unknowable future, we must embrace the wisdom of the East and the West as we had Ranga and Uncle R. B. We had discovered why we had to change. We did not only want to survive.

We wanted to thrive.

Troy Knowlton
Operations Manager
and
Jimmy Spurger
Pre-Production Manager

First Impressions

Troy: I've been here since 1956. I hired on at age 17 as part of my high school job training. Never asked for a raise and never asked for a day off, except when my child was born.

Because of an event that happened a couple of years ago, Dale said he'd make me a deal. He said I was too important to lose. He let me take every Thursday off to unwind. That kind of caring reminds me of Dale's Uncle R. B., a very Christian man. He taught us all a lot. Miss him everyday.

Jimmy: My uncle got me my job here when I was 16. That's 40 years ago. He was married to Roy's sister. At the time I was down to my last pair of jeans. Really needed the job.

"Mr. C" (I never called him Roy) was always very fair. Never promised a lot, but if I did the work, he said I'd have a place here. Since I really had no father, Mr. C was the father I would have wanted. Never reprimanded me that I didn't deserve it. He hears me out. We're "Dad's people," that's what Dale calls us.

The Quest for Quality

Troy: At first I wondered where this was going to take us? Could we get there? I tried to understand it. Dale said you don't have to agree, just try to understand it. It was expensive too. Time away from production is an expense. But we've progressed so far in the last three years that we now have multi-million dollar companies asking us how we do it!

Jimmy: Dale had made Troy and me co-production managers in 1989. We got everything the way we wanted it in production. We had a real comfort zone. Then Dale brings in his quest for quality. I thought it stunk.

The more I studied it, the more I realized the big change is really in the management of process and not so much changing the procedures. I definitely think it's for the better now.

The Flow of Influence

Troy: When we were all younger, we influenced Dale a lot. Now he's a big influence on us. His leadership qualities have surfaced. He got support from people because he worked, not because he was the boss's son.

When he proposed the quest, it was difficult to see. There were risks: you lose some people, stress level was in the red zone. It was a gutsy call on Dale's part. The decision to go with quality takes you to another level. It took me a year to think it could work.

Jimmy: We were trained in conservatism by Mr. C. The proof's in the pudding. It was more difficult for Dale to tell us older guys.

The Malcolm Baldrige Award

Troy: My goal is to get better, not to win the Malcolm Baldrige Award. The learning from applying for the award makes us better. We analyze everything we do now. We may not win the Award, but the idea is to get better, not bigger.

I've been to several of these quality schools, one of them at the Hogan Center. One time a participant asked me, "When are they going to tell us how to do this?" And I said, "They're not going to tell you how to do it. But they are going to tell you what needs to be done. You need to apply it to your own organization. They're not going to tell you to do this and this and this. You take a look at everything they present and ask yourself how would this work in your application."

To have a plan is the basic thing. You have to take it in steps or stages. If you look at it and try to do it all at once, then you've got problems.

We follow the Baldrige criteria for our business plan, but we don't follow it exactly. We adapt it to our business.

If we followed everything to the letter, we may end up like some of the companies who are just out to try to win the Baldrige. They don't win the Award and they don't improve either. That's no plan. We apply the Baldrige criteria as a business plan for us to improve. And we've definitely improved.

Personal Impact

Jimmy: I was in serious financial trouble and my health wasn't the best in the world. So I set myself a goal, in case something happened to me, that I would leave my wife with a home paid off and without a lot of bills.

Today my wife has a home that's paid for, all of our vehicles and everything we own is paid for, there's not one bill, and there's a nest egg in the bank. It's enough to live on.

All this just by setting goals and sticking with it and doing what needs to be done. I did it in five years. It was our own quality journey.

Look, this is not rocket science. When you break it down it's just as simple as it can be. It's only when you try to look at the whole conglomerate that it can be overwhelming.

TELLING
THE TALE

Embracing the wisdom of the East and the West became my personal challenge. Ranga had encouraged me to go back to school and finish my college degree. And shortly before he died, he had convinced me to attend examiner training for the Texas Quality Award.

The significance of these two recommendations can not be understated. Were it not for Ranga encouraging me to go back to school, I might never have found a friend and an idea that together have enabled all of our employees to share in the financial gains of Texas Nameplate.

Were it not for Ranga convincing me to attend examiner training, I might never have made two other friends and understood so clearly the seven essential drivers that ensure our success at Texas Nameplate, whether or not we win awards.

But, were it not also for Uncle R. B.'s Christian influence, I might not have chosen LeTourneau University where evening courses are offered in business as well as in Christianity and Scripture. It proved to be an excellent choice.

The influence of these two quality mentors had survived their deaths. And I was about to take the quest for quality to a more deeply personal level, with telling results.

As you might imagine, it was not easy going back to school. At 43, I was usually one of the oldest students in class. I was not used to all the studying and reading we had to do. Nor was my family used to me working all day and then working all night.

Clearly, if you can go to college when you're young, it's better because of the energy required and the lack of other commitments. On the other hand, unlike some of the younger students, I knew more about the usefulness of what I was learning. I was constantly thinking about how I could apply what I learned to the conduct of our business.

I was also a little better judge of character in the friends I chose to hang around with. One of those "characters" was Scott Weber. We became good friends, particularly after taking an accounting class together. That is where I ran into the idea of gainsharing or sharing with employees the gains the company made by their increasing efficiency. After Scott joined us at Texas Nameplate, he helped me implement the idea.

The proverb "better late than never" was especially true, not only for my college degree, but also for what gainsharing came to mean to Texas Nameplate and its employees.

During this same time, I also took the Texas Quality Award examiner training. On the first day of training, with about 100 people present, we were asked to stand up and introduce ourselves and tell why we were qualified to be an examiner.

Everybody before me mentioned all their quality accomplishments like "Quality Control Manager for EDS, with a certificate in Quality Engineering and Statistics" or "five years on the quality examiner board for Texaco Oil," for example.

When it was my turn, I was so scared, I just stood up, told them my name, said I was president of Texas Nameplate Company in Dallas, and sat back down.

I did not know at the time that I was the only president of any organization taking the three-day course. To this day, I still wonder whether a company is really committed to the quality process if the company's president has not committed the time for such courses.

At the training, I met two people who would help Texas Nameplate and take up where Ranga and Uncle R. B. left off.

The first was a fellow by the name of Barry Johnson, a former IBMer, a quality consultant and Malcolm Baldrige examiner. The second person was Jackie Kennett, also a quality consultant and Baldrige examiner. Among many other qualities, she was an excellent application writer. Since that first meeting at the training, we have all become best of friends.

Barry ended up helping us a lot with our applications for the Texas Quality Award and also for the Malcolm Baldrige Award.

I asked Jackie to help us write our application for the upcoming Texas Quality Award and she agreed.

With the examiner training behind us,

we started the long, hard process of writing. It took us over seven months and countless drafts. Mainly it was Bob Mantle, Troy Knowlton, Jackie and I who would come down to the office just about every other Saturday to work on it. We kept working on our weaknesses and assuring our strengths.

Believe it or not, at no time did we ever talk about winning the Texas Quality Award. It was like an unspoken rule. We were focused almost exclusively on learning how the Texas Quality Award criteria would help our business.

In these sessions, we really learned how to use the criteria to improve our business and we all learned a lot from Jackie. She was very patient with us and helped us learn that we should never do anything "just because" of the award criteria. We learned to use them only if they were applicable to our business.

As I described in the prologue, it was during this time that we discovered our seven business drivers. They became an essential part of our application. But our application could not rely just on these reasons for doing business.

Our next task was to prepare the most objective facts we could to support our application. In general, it was a three-step process. First, we had to sort through all the available data looking for the most informative pieces. Second, we had to select from the resulting information only the most significant facts that supported our claim to fulfill the criteria. Third, we had to determine how best to depict these facts so our readers could learn them quickly.

Charting Our Quality Journey

The charts I've included here are like those you would find in our application, but they are not the same because they include time periods after the competition. Thus they show trends we successfully predicted in 1996.

1. Metal Nameplate Market Share

The first chart, on the following page, shows the growing market share that Texas Nameplate has enjoyed over the four-year period during which we began our quest for quality.

Every time I look at this chart, I remember my drive into Texas Nameplate that fateful morning when I heard the statistics of third-generation family businesses not making it.

And to think, I had to ramrod us out of that likely problem by using a statistical process control program I didn't want to accept. The irony of it all is right there on the chart.

2. Sales Growth

The second chart signals a trend that Bob Mantle is largely responsible for. It shows how strong our sales growth has been as compared to our competition.

Now obviously, figures like these are neat to look at when they are so positive. But we have learned in our quest for quality that they are really the signs of how our ordinary world changed as a result of everything we have

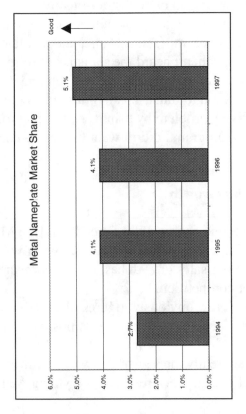

Metal Nameplate Market Share

Percent of Market compared against years indicated.

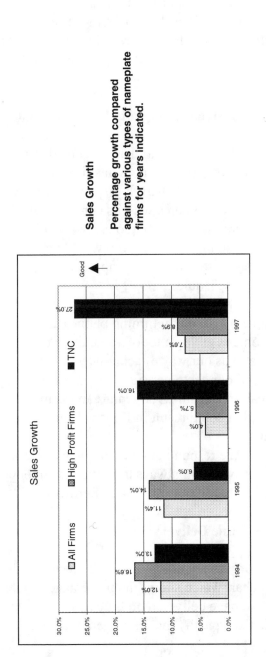

Sales Growth

Percentage growth compared against various types of nameplate firms for years indicated.

done to improve our business. We don't rely just on our market share or our sales to measure quality. We see them as two of the indicators of what happens when quality is achieved in the marketplace.

3. Responsiveness – Quote Response Time

If you ask customers what quality means to them, you get measurements like those we depict on the next chart. It displays how Texas Nameplate compares with its competition when customers ask for a job quote. By providing a timely response to those who would be our customers we are showing our appreciation of their business schedules.

We look at quote response time as more than being good at returning phone calls, which for some is giving a lot of value these days. We look at it as our way of acknowledging what many of our customers undoubtedly are feeling: the call to a business adventure in the market place that could result in financial success all around.

We respond quickly to quote requests because we want always to participate in opportunities that fit our own plan of growth.

4. On-Time Delivery

Our concern about time is also reflected in the next chart which shows the percentage of jobs that we have delivered on time by our standard, which is typically more stringent than our cus-

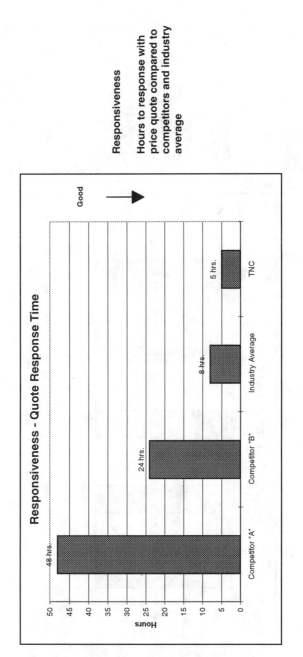

Responsiveness

Hours to response with price quote compared to competitors and industry average

Responsiveness - Quote Response Time

Good

Hours

Competitor "A"   48 hrs.
Competitor "B"   24 hrs.
Industry Average 8 hrs.
TNC   5 hrs.

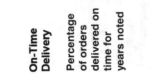

On-Time Delivery

Percentage of orders delivered on time for years noted

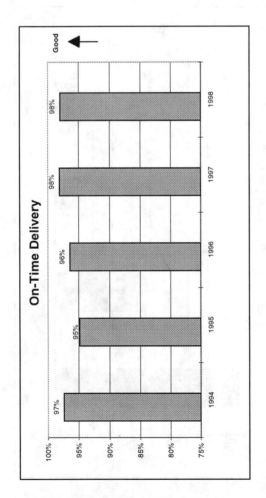

tomers' standard. With a goal of 95%, we continue to surpass it year after year.

5. Complaints / Orders Shipped

Of course, just because we have delivered the jobs on time doesn't necessarily mean that we have no complaints. The next chart shows our progress in this important area.

During the two years depicted, our percentage of complaints per orders shipped was dramatically lower than both the industry's and comparable competitors' percentages.

As most businesses know, customers are no longer reluctant to complain. At Texas Nameplate we have likewise changed our attitudes about complaints as well, ever since we started looking at quality. We now look forward to dealing with complaints when we get them because they give us notice of areas we can improve.

There will be some who don't buy this attitude about quality and improvement. Texas Nameplate did not always have this attitude. But we are not saying the quest for quality is just an attitude fix.

Unfortunately, most businesses may need something more than a change in attitude. They may need what we discovered when we first started applying statistics to our processes and tried to get control of them.

Complaints per Order Shipped

Percentages compared to industry, competiors, and self for years indicated

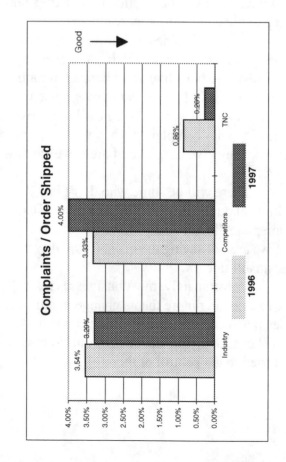

Complaints / Order Shipped

6. Overruns

The next chart, depicting overruns as a percentage of pieces of nameplates made, tells a much more interesting, even compelling, story about the wisdom of pursuing the quality journey and taking it to the next level.

On the face of it, what you see here are several years of smaller and smaller percentages of overruns.

The significance of the chart may not be immediately as obvious as quote response times and delivery times. It may not be as impressive as market share or even sales growth.

But at the heart of it, these figures are equally, if not more important, for they speak of how Texas Nameplate took dead aim at its costs of doing business and hit a key target.

By lowering the amount of overruns that are needed to fulfill a job, we no longer, for example, have to make 1120 pieces in order to deliver 1000 quality pieces. We now would run only 1040. Since Texas Nameplate ships millions of nameplates yearly, reducing our overruns means higher quality and lower cost.

While the overrun situation can be turned around using quality processes that can be statistically measured, the question naturally arises, and certainly did at Texas Nameplate, at what price?

We're not talking just about cost savings. We're talking about employees and the price we and they pay for taking up the quest for quality.

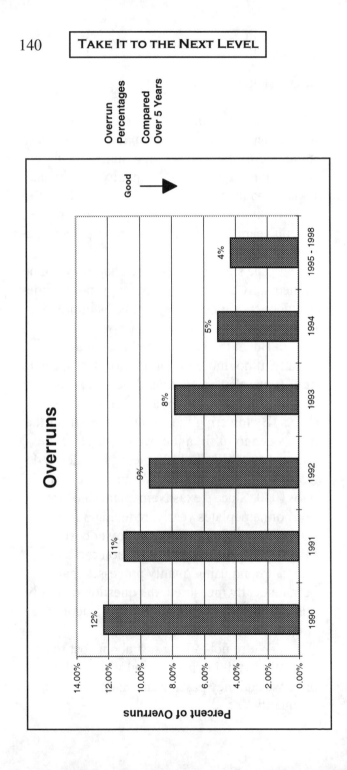

Overrun Percentages
Compared Over 5 Years

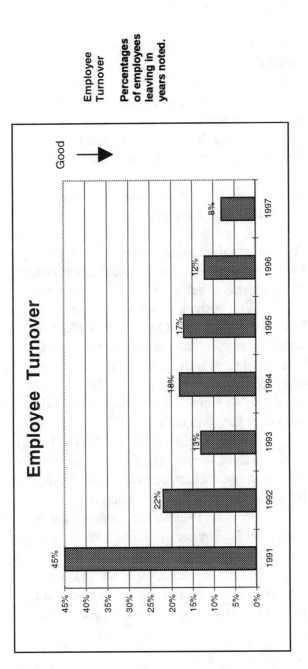

Employee Turnover

Percentages of employees leaving in years noted.

7. Employee Turnover

I am happy to report on the next chart that, rather than increasing our turnover rate, this commitment to working with each other to achieve quality products actually lowered our turnover substantially.

During the years noted, you can readily see that our employees are staying with us.

8a. Average Total Compensation Per Production Employee

As an internal measure of our success, we regularly survey our employees to better gauge how they feel about various aspects of their work.

We ask them whether the instruction we have given them about their jobs is adequate, whether they feel their work is appreciated, whether their work conditions are satisfactory, whether they feel involved with Texas Nameplate, and whether they are satisfied overall with their jobs and their salary.

As you might expect, our survey results continue to be very positive. When we take a look at the next chart, one of the most important bases for this satisfaction is depicted.

This chart shows the average total compensation figures per production level employee over the last five years.

As I trust you can see, we've come a long way in this crucial area of demonstrating to our employees how much we appreciate them.

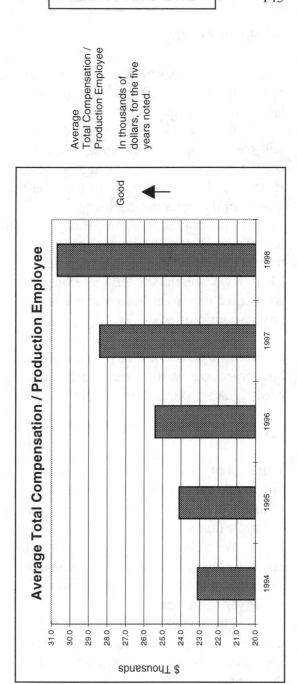

Average
Total Compensation /
Production Employee

In thousands of
dollars, for the five
years noted.

8b. Water Quality

As an external measure of our success, we look at something quite different than employee satisfaction and compensation.

When you look at the next chart, you will see the continuing progress Texas Nameplate is making in improving another of the most crucial by-products of our processes: the quality of the water we discharge.

This is a far cry from our days in court with Texas Water Utilities and the Environmental Protection Agency ten years ago. Though we won those cases on technicalities, we learned important lessons about our community responsibilities.

Since the EPA standard is 1.220 milligrams of suspended metals per liter of water discharged, our waste water, at only 0.033, exceeds EPA standards dramatically.

9. Cycle Time

While all of these previous measurements are important in themselves, for our customers one of the most critical measures of our quality is our cycle time.

With cycle time we keep track of the number of days it takes us to go through an entire cycle of the process, from taking a job order to delivering the job.

The next chart shows how Texas Nameplate has lowered this cycle time and stayed consistently lower than competitors and the industry average.

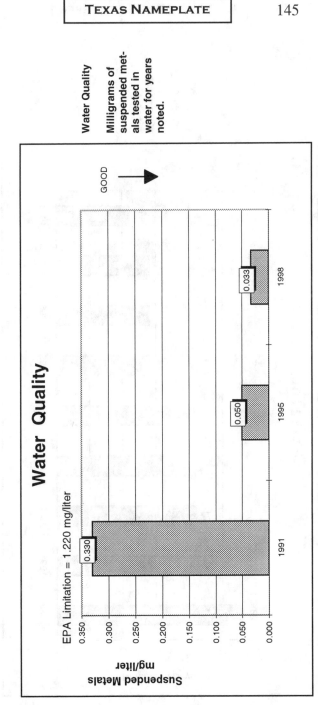

Water Quality

Milligrams of suspended metals tested in water for years noted.

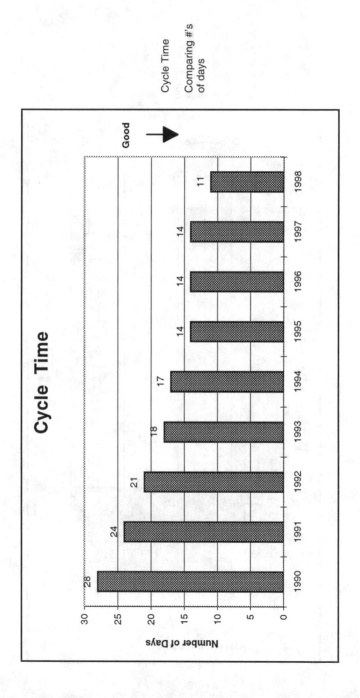

Cycle Time
Comparing #'s
of days

We have set ambitious goals in this area to reduce the cycle time even further without sacrificing quality.

10. Nonconformances

With cycle time reduced, we're pleased and proud to show you the results of our work to reduce nonconformances. The next chart shows the levels of such measures.

The bottom line shows "customer nonconformances." By this we mean the defects that our customers have reported to us. We are very pleased with this trend.

But, it is also important to note our "total nonconformances." Here we are able to show our progress in catching our own problems, even ones that our customers would never see.

By either measure, our nonconformances, or defects, have been reduced substantially during our quest for quality. We believe the two go hand in hand.

11a. Units per Hour

Now I know there are some bottom-liners out there who have been patiently waiting to get to these next two charts.

The first chart I present depicts the number of units of nameplates per hour of labor performed. In a general way, this chart shows bottom-line productivity. During the five years noted, you can see the trend to more productiv-

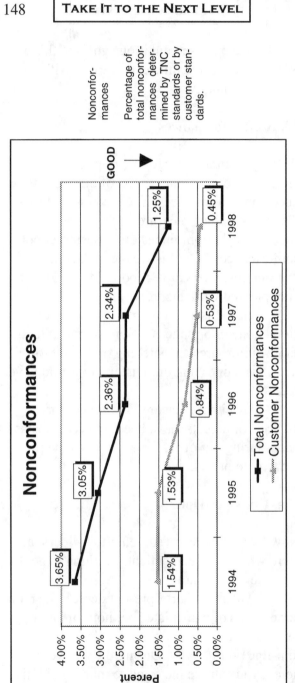

Nonconformances

Percentage of total nonconformances determined by TNC standards or by customer standards.

ity. Coupled with our trends to better quality, this chart almost says it all. We are producing more with better quality than ever before.

11b. Gross Profit

Without this next chart, however, the concerns of the bottom-liners are still not addressed. Dad especially likes this one. And from a bottom-line perspective, this chart has to be one of the most convincing charts to show how quality can be profitable.

When you look at gross profit and compare it to the cost of Texas Nameplate's sales over the five years noted, you will see our gross profits grow and grow, while our cost of sales go down and down. Moreover, you would be as pleased as we are to learn that these figures outperform competitors and the industry average.

12. Partners for Success

Our final chart shows a major consequence of all of those that I have described thus far.

When we show prospective customers the measurements of our:

- Metal Nameplate Market Share
- Sales Growth
- Responsiveness – Quote Response Time
- On-Time Delivery
- Complaints per Orders Shipped
- Overruns
- Employee Turnover

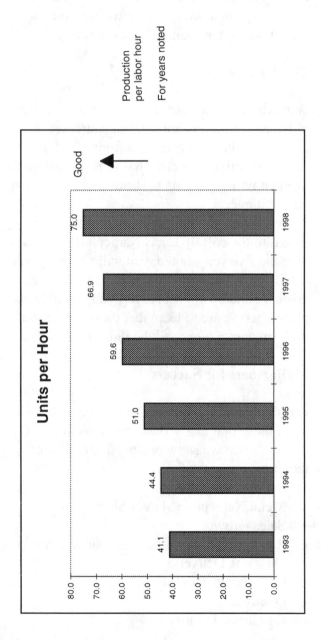

Production
per labor hour

For years noted

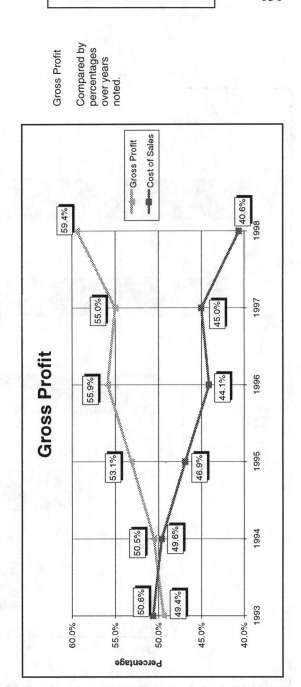

Gross Profit

Compared by
percentages
over years
noted.

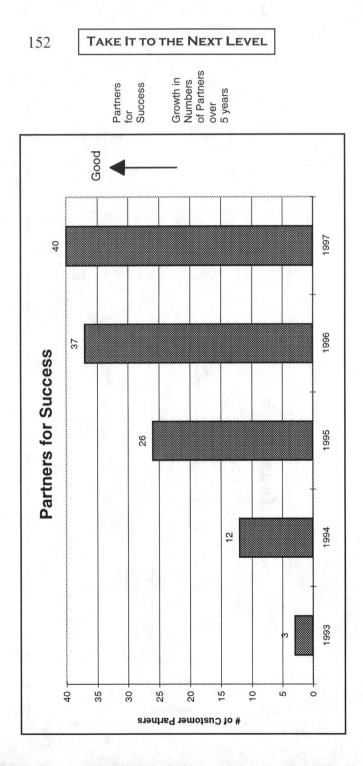

Partners
for
Success

Growth in
Numbers
of Partners
over
5 years

- Average Total Compensation per Production Employee and Water quality
- Cycle Time
- Nonconformances, and
- Units per Hour and Gross Profits,

our invitation for them to join our most comprehensive customer service program is most readily accepted.

When we show them this final chart, it reveals the destination of the quality journey for Texas Nameplate.

Our Partners for Success program enables our key customers to work with us in this manner to mutually plan for nameplate needs over a longer period of time.

Not only do they have the opportunity to lock in extremely competitive prices, but also Texas Nameplate has the opportunity to achieve its strategic plans, in the short and long term, with a high degree of predictability.

By November 1, 1995, with the enormous help of Sula Reilly, who did all the typing and formatting, we were ready to submit our application for the 1996 cycle of the Texas Quality Award.

When we submitted our application, the only question left in our minds was whether the judges would see it our way.

The answer they gave surprised us all.

Scott Weber
Director of Administration

Baldrige Criteria and Business

"Adopting the criteria brought in new areas of challenges, strategic plans for example. We never really had them in the past. Looking at capability studies. We never did that before. Looking at process improvements, being able to deploy the criteria and have supervisors take ownership. This was all new. But it saves money."

Gainsharing

"Dale and I met when we were both going back to finish our college degrees. We were in a class together and the idea of gainsharing came up. I could see Dale's wheels turning. He said to me, 'Wouldn't that be neat to give some of the savings from process improvement back to the employees?' I drove home that night saying to myself, 'Give it back?!?!'

"When we gave our first four quarters of gainsharing, it was approximately $2,700 extra per employee, $180,000 altogether. That would have been money wasted with nonconformances (defects). But Dale and Mr. C were willing to share this "gain," because after all, it meant we didn't have to purchase excess materials.

"When I first looked at this, I have to admit I fought it. I saw that our profit and loss statement was taking a hit for whatever the gainsharing amount was. It showed up on our income statement as a separate expense item. Dale would look at it and say, 'No, we didn't have an expense. We're sharing savings.'

"It took a while for me to see it. Finally it clicked one day. This is just a reclassification because we do not have to put money into materials purchased. When it's in materials purchased, because we buy materials in volume, we're not using the money as fast. The inventory is there and we're able to produce the product without having to go back and purchase more in a volatile market. That could cost us thousands each quarter.

"Now, rather than a possible bonus at the end of the year, eligible employees get four gainsharing checks per year based on performance. So chances are our billings and profits are higher. They have been thus far."

DON'T KISS
THE TROPHY

My best friend for many years has been Roy
Basa. He's a lot of fun, has a great attitude
about life, and taught me not to hang around
anybody with a bad one.

Roy and I met in 1971 when I attended
the University of Texas at Arlington. I talked
him into joining our fraternity, Sigma Phi Epsi-
lon, and I was his "big brother" for two years.
We later lived together while attending college
as well as after I had left school to work at
Texas Nameplate. We basically grew up together during those years.

Friends like Roy are hard workers, trustworthy, loyal, understanding, sincere and very
much family-oriented. They are few and far between.

When we entered the competition for
the Texas Quality Award, we didn't expect our
application to be read by friends like Roy, nor
for that matter by people like a former friend we
painfully remembered.

We hoped for an objective read from
judges who had no axe to grind, like some of
our senior people years earlier. We hoped for
constructive criticism from judges who shared
an interest in our future, unlike some family
members who shared none.

Since you have already learned about
the seven forces that drive Texas Nameplate

and the many facts that supported our application, I think you probably understand why we believed that, if the judges were people like Roy, they would be proud of what we had accomplished on our quest for quality.

Likewise, I think you probably understand why we believed that if the judges were people like my former high school buddy, they would probably be in denial. If they were like the employees who covertly challenged our efforts, they would be almost dumbfounded. And if they were like some of my family members, they might someday admit they were impressed, but not any day soon.

In some ways, submitting the application reminded me of when Roy and I were applying for membership in the fraternity. But this time the stakes were considerably higher and the membership was much more highly selective.

During January 1996, following our November 1995 submission of the application, we started working on a possible site visit by the Texas Quality Award examiners. In February we received a call indicating we were indeed going to receive one. We were all very excited.

The site visit for the Texas Quality Award was really neat. All of our employees finally got a chance to see their hard work examined.

Then there was the wait following the site visit. It was not an easy time. We had exposed ourselves to a lot of probing questions, far beyond our own soul-searching. And then, after what seemed to be years, but was actually just a few months, the judges' answer came.

Texas Nameplate had won the 1996 Texas Quality Award.

The feelings all of us had when we learned of this are almost beyond description. For me, the thrill of learning about it went through my whole body like an electrical charge. It's like what you might feel if you were a golfer and you hit a hole in one. Even though you know it happened, because you just saw it happen, you still don't believe it.

While we knew it might happen, the shock of it actually happening was what was surprising.

We were told that the awards program would be held in June in Austin, the capitol of the State of Texas.

I was so thrilled that I made the easy and quick decision to take all the Texas Nameplate employees to the awards ceremony. When that wonderful day came around, we all boarded a bus and drove the 200 miles south to Austin.

Once at the ceremony, we all watched as other companies, including one or two local Austin companies, got up to receive their awards. While the recipients were cordial and appreciative, it seemed that the award did not mean as much to them as ours did to us. We had shut down our entire plant and driven 200 miles for this event.

When I was called up to receive the award, I was deeply moved to be able to stand up in front of everyone present, but most importantly, in front of all of the employees of Texas Nameplate, and receive the award on behalf of all of us.

I happily gave credit to them, saying it was a indeed a privilege to work with such a dedicated group of people who had achieved such significant recognition for the quality of their work. Little did we all know that our mutual letter of commitment signed only a few years before would have led to this.

I loved having our picture taken with all of the employees, including Dad and me, holding the Texas Quality Award trophy.

It meant so much to me to share this award with Dad, given all that we had been through to get there, and to again acknowledge his faith in me to let me pursue the quest for quality.

As we drove back from the Austin awards ceremony, I felt extremely confident in my judgment to have already submitted our application to enter the competition for that year's Malcolm Baldrige Award.

For, you see, as soon as we heard we had won the Texas Quality Award, I immediately contacted Jackie Kennett about writing our first Baldrige application.

Since it was due immediately after we went down to the Texas Quality Awards ceremony, we all had worked really, really hard on this one. We only had two months to put it together.

Jackie really did not want to do this application for reasons more obvious to me now than then. To put it mildly, I suppose you might say we were a bit cocky after our Texas Quality Award win.

Though Jackie was pregnant at the time, she let me talk her into it. She was most generous under the circumstances and went on to deliver not only a great first application, but a healthy baby boy for her first child.

My objective was to keep the momentum going after the Texas Quality Award. I was still afraid some of our people might slow down or lose interest in the process after we won the award.

More important to me, I wanted the Baldrige feedback to compare with the Texas Quality Award feedback. The comparison would be telling and the feedback crucial to our continuing efforts to improve.

When we did not receive a Baldrige site visit in 1996, we were not too terribly upset. Our application had been rushed and we were still under the influence of the euphoria of winning the state award. But we also recognized that we were playing with the big boys now.

As a result of winning the Texas Quality Award, we started receiving a lot of recognition, I supposed mainly because Texas Nameplate was so small and nobody had ever heard of us before. We also have Warren Hogan, of the Hogan Center, to thank for spreading the word about us.

From June of 1996, the month we were honored with the Texas Quality Award, until the end of December 1996, Texas Nameplate representatives, including one of our most trusted employees, Robert Hodge, Jr., gave many presentations throughout Texas on what we had been able to accomplish on our quest for quality.

In September of 1996, we were elated to receive ISO 9002 certification. (See *Glossary*.) We were only one of three U.S. nameplate companies to be so certified.

Later that fall, we got the feedback from the judges of both the Texas Quality and Malcolm Baldrige Awards. From the feedback we learned that we still really had a long way to go. It was clear in both reports that we still needed trend data and we still needed to work on our strategic planning process. So we began immediately to work on the feedback.

Starting in January 1997, we were able to implement our first price adjustment since 1992. Dad liked this idea a lot. Working with measurements of our true costs and customer satisfaction, we felt confident that the timing of our price adjustment was perfect. It went so well that we did not lose any of our top 50 customers, even though we raised our prices quite a bit.

During February we applied for the Texas Association of Businesses and Chambers of Commerce (TABCC) Private Business of the Year award. Warren Hogan brought this to our attention, since we had no prior knowledge of it. Barry Johnson wrote this application because we had already gotten Jackie to start work on our second Baldrige application.

In March, Texas Nameplate was named winner of the prestigious TABCC award, winning over 16 other private companies.

Barry also wrote our application that spring for Arthur Andersen's Best Practices Award in the areas of customer satisfaction and employee retention and morale. Texas Nameplate won in both categories and advanced to the international level of competition as well.

Since it was part of our strategic plan to start our gainsharing plan during 1997, we implemented it in April.

By the time we began gainsharing with eligible employees, and that was all of them, our people showed all the signs of understanding the rewards of their efforts.

We were definitely on a roll. Sales picked up. Profits picked up. Even a delegation from Pohang Iron & Steel in South Korea, the world's second largest steel maker, came to visit us. Their college-professor guide said they wanted to benchmark us in their own quest for quality.

In May 1997, we submitted our second and best Baldrige application. Ever since I kissed the trophy in Washington D.C. at the Baldrige Quest, I had waited for this day. I felt sure Texas Nameplate would bring the trophy home. So confident were we, that we began work on a possible site visit in early June of 1997.

In August, our confidence was confirmed. We learned that we were one of only three small businesses in the U.S. to receive the go-ahead for a site visit.

We were having fun at this point.

The mood was exhilarating. All of us at Texas Nameplate were having a great time preparing for the coming site visit. As hosts, we were ready to put on a Texas welcome like they had never seen before.

When the site visit team came to see us, in the second week of September 1997, the visit was a blast. The team members were neat people and they seemed to thoroughly enjoy their stay with us that week.

Given how encouraging the week was, we expected nothing less than the most favorable of comments from the Baldrige examiner team after they left. We waited for the examiners to make their reports, expecting only great news.

I finally got the call in October, telling us we had not won. It hurt. I hurt, big time. "I shouldn't have kissed the trophy," I said to myself. "God only knows what we will do now to take it to the next level."

Dale Crownover
President
Thoughts on Leadership

Whenever I find myself in a decision-making situation, I always try to remember what it means to me to take on the responsibilities of leadership. Here's a brief summary of what I go over in my mind when I make key decisions.

Be a Player
We learn from our mistakes. It is better to strike out than to never step into the batter's box.

Know the Real Issue
Winning is not the goal, getting better is. For example, our primary goal on the quest for quality is to receive a site visit. Feedback is so much more relevant and important after a site visit. They're also a lot of fun.

Stand Up to Adversity
Adversity brings out the best in us. Have faith and confidence in ourselves and others we trust. What may seem to be bad at the moment, may be a blessing for the future.

Accept the Gift of Challenges
View each challenge as an opportunity, but even more as a gift. Then visualize success. Do our best but especially be patient while we pursue our vision or dream.

Set Goals Early, Then Keep Focused

Set goals – some easy, some harder, some almost impossible yet obtainable. Then be consistent with your approach and deployment, every day and with every decision. Keep focused and the results will come. It's elementary, just not obvious.

Be Choosy and Take Powerful Measures

You are who you hang with. Be choosy when it comes to your friends and those you love. They are the ones who will help you get to the next level. Talking with them gives you a better sense of yourself. Work with them to take powerful measures. Learn to love data. Data is great. It helps you prioritize, set standards, and measure achievement. Measure everything at least once to find out how important or unimportant that particular function or process step is. Then use what you measure.

Take Feedback to Heart

Seek feedback and learn how to accept constructive criticism and even, sometimes, harsh criticism. It's very difficult to improve processes if you can't accept feedback. Learn from those who have been there and are willing to help. Don't lose heart. Listen, learn and try your best. Never lose the desire to become better at what you are trying to accomplish. And don't hurry. Remember the only truly wrong thing to do is do nothing.

Lead by Being Led
One thing that can never be taken away from us is our education. Be willing to learn and never consider ourselves too old to learn. Get our degrees. It doesn't matter when, but get at least one. It provides not only the education we want but it contributes to the self-esteem we need to continue the quest.

Make Decisions
As leaders, we must first examine our own assumptions and seek the views of others whom we respect and admire before we make decisions that affect others. We keep the best interest of the group at heart and take all the time we need to assess pros, cons, repercussions, and even the "worst case scenario." If we can deal with what we judge to be the worst – if it were to happen as a result of our decision – we will be ready to make the decision at the right time.

Persuade Others to Embrace the Change
Half the people at work like change, a fourth take a wait-and-see approach, and the other fourth do not want to change. It is not easy for anybody to change old habits. Be very patient. Tell people there is nothing wrong with the way they've been doing things. There may be a better way of doing it. Put yourself in their shoes. We all need each other. Let them make the decision to be willing to change. Don't tell, suggest.

The Paradox of Losing; the Time to Decide
We never lose if we never try to win. Be a good

loser. Anybody can be a good winner. Life is a three-sixty [360°] — we have to look at everything. There is a reason for everything. Accept what God has provided. We do not have to agree but we have to accept. When we've looked at everything and asked ourselves the ramifications for others of our decisions, we're ready to decide.

Share
Share company recognition with all our employees. And share everything possible with our family. People want to help us. They will, both mentally and physically, especially if we share.

 # MR. BALDRIGE, MEET THE NEXT GENERATION

I can only remember crying twice in my adult life. The first time, I cried tears of sadness when Uncle R. B. died. The second time, I cried tears of joy when I graduated from LeTourneau University in 1997. Finally.

I didn't have it in me to cry over the Baldrige results, though it might have done me some good. Instead, I withdrew a little at first.

I sat at my desk thinking of one of the only poems I ever liked in high school. It was by Robert Frost. The final line of *The Road Not Taken* is what most people still remember. It goes like this:

> "Two roads diverged
> in a wood, and I -
> I took the one
> less traveled by,
> And that has made
> all the difference."

I began to wonder whether we had taken Texas Nameplate not only down a road less traveled, but maybe down a dead-end road. What we did now in the face of this disappointing news would surely make all the difference.

Of course, I had tried to prepare everyone at the office in case we got bad news, though none of us really expected it.

When I made the announcement to the Texas Nameplate employees, everyone seemed to take it reasonably well. We all still had our game-faces on, I suppose.

But I could tell some were looking at me closely to see how I was really taking the "loss." I steeled myself from taking it too hard or any deeper than was necessary. This wasn't too hard because I did not see this as a failure on anyone's part.

Remembering Ranga's kaleidoscope, I realized that what counted was largely a matter of how we were going to look at this turn of events.

Remembering Uncle R. B., I realized that fear of any kind was useless under the circumstances. As Jesus often said to his disciples, what was needed was trust. After all, losing the Malcolm Baldrige Award was not like the challenge Job encountered when God tested him.

But I was concerned that some among us would take the "loss" too much to heart and become discouraged.

I needed to act quickly to interpret the significance of this event so our employees could avoid any self-defeating, if not self-destructive, behaviors. We didn't need this loss to hurt us at work or at home.

For some, our calm, non-defensive response worked well enough. There may have even been some who hoped that things would get back to normal, the way they used to be, now that we had tried this quest and had come up short.

For others, though, more support was needed. We hadn't come all this way to miss the point of the competition.

So, for a while in the aftermath of the news, I had to let myself hang on the paradox of it all for as long as I could take it. By this, I mean I had to tell us all, including myself, in one way or another, that "losers" always miss the point of the competition, even though they may win it, while "winners" always get the point of the competition, even though they lose it.

But after getting the wind knocked out of our sails, I thought it best to take it easy for a while. For me I felt like heading back home. So, at the end of the day I began my long drive.

It was a much different drive than the one I had started some eight years before where I began this story. During that drive, remember, I was struck by what I heard on the radio about the odds against third generations succeeding with family-owned businesses. This time I was facing the consequences for the family of bucking the odds against winning the Malcolm Baldrige Award.

Eight years ago, I didn't know I was driving into a situation where General Dynamics was about to change our lives by demanding that we initiate statistical process controls for nameplate production. I didn't know what situation I was driving into this time, either, when I headed home. But I was driving into something, and it would change our lives just as much.

In hindsight I would have to say, I was about to pass through an understandable moment of despair after the Baldrige results were made public. But simply to say that does not do it justice. I want to describe it more fully so if you ever find yourself driving down that road, you'll see it coming.

It began when it hit me how hard we had worked to get to this point, only to be told we hadn't won.

Undoubtedly, my heroes had faced these moments. Surely Coach Tom Landry and Roger Staubach had known defeat on the playing fields after hard-fought battles. Both my grandfather and Dad knew despair during their lifetimes and they made it through.

Perhaps this was going to be my time to experience the full brunt of such despair. I wasn't sure what I was going to do to take Texas Nameplate to the next level. Forgive my French, but hell, I wasn't even sure what the next step was, let alone what the next level might be.

I knew it wasn't going to be easy telling Mom and Dad. This was not the time for me to play the prodigal son, though. Admittedly, a lot of money had been spent on the Baldrige effort. But it had not been squandered by any means. We had learned a lot — and in the process Texas Nameplate benefited enormously.

Still, I knew it wasn't going to be any easier telling Julie and my boys. After taking so many hours away from them and after raising all their hopes, what was I going to say to the next generation of Crownovers about the true meaning of this "loss" ?

I knew that if I told them all as quickly and as matter-of-factly as possible, they would be understanding and be ready to support me. I would appreciate that for sure.

But as I drove along the highway, I realized I had been given an opportunity to do more than simply pass this "loss" off as an insignificant bump in the road.

I began to think more and more about my children, Texas Nameplate's next generation, and about what I could tell them about such moments of despair. I wanted to do a little benchmarking on how to handle feelings of depression that sometimes all of us have to deal with in life, but maybe especially in the world of small business.

I started by remembering when I was their age. One of my sources of near-despair for the longest time was not knowing I could be my own person. Despite Mom and Dad's repeated advice, for example, about my relationship to my brother, it took me a long time to come out from under his influence. I suppose neither my brother nor I could have known any better than to be the way we were. At that young an age, we couldn't be expected to have an adult's understanding of why or how we were so different in personalities and attitudes.

When I had finally had enough of Doug's ways and decided to let him have some of mine, I passed through that moment of despair, but perhaps at the expense of a close relationship to my only brother.

I certainly didn't want that kind of bad feeling to come between my own two sons. It saddens me that it still exists between Doug and me.

Yet, I had to pass through a similar moment of near-despair later in life. I remembered how I felt before I finally got Dad to let me have the bigger role and set of responsibilities that came with becoming president of Texas Nameplate.

Of course, I didn't resort to hitting him in the head with a stick like I did with my brother when we were little. And the consequence had been just the opposite. Dad and I had become much closer these last eight years.

I could also tell my children that, when I was a little older, I often really wanted to be someone other than myself. You might say this was my hero-worship phase. And though I listened to a lot of advice from my different heroes, the hardest thing for me to do was to get past wanting to be them rather than be me.

Similar moments of this kind of despair happened during Texas Nameplate's quest for quality and the Malcolm Baldrige Award.

Fortunately, I knew enough about this type of problem to give my friends at Texas Nameplate and elsewhere free rein to bring me back down to earth whenever I needed the grounding.

Lastly, I could tell my children that, when I was a teenager, I had to confront yet an-

other kind of despair. This was the most difficult one of all.

I had to get past what every teenage boy
and girl wants: just to be myself, to be left
alone, to have things my own way. This was
tough. I had to learn how not to be egotistical or
egocentric without losing the good part of my
ego in the process. For a teenager, that was and
still is a tall order.

Fortunately for me and for those around
me, it was about this time that I decided to take
seriously the most unselfish man I had ever
come across. I became a believer in Jesus
Christ. He became my Way, my Truth, and my
Life. My decision to follow Him made all the
difference at that time of my life.

Then it hit me. Could this present moment of despair over not winning the Malcolm
Baldrige Award be a test of my present level of
faith? Maybe Uncle R. B. had been right about
this quest for quality.

Maybe "going for the gold" like Ranga
and others called it, was just another form of
ego-stroking. In football, giant egos still seek
the Vince Lombardi trophy at the Super Bowl.
In Hollywood, ego-driven stars still seek their
Oscars at the Academy Awards.

Perhaps the Baldrige Award and the
Texas Quality Award were little more than vain
trophies for unsuspecting businessmen, what
Moses might have called smaller versions of the
"golden calf."

I caught myself. Despair like pessimism,
even if only momentary, can quickly dis-

integrate even the most faithful of men and women. It can produce a form of cynicism that is like quicksand for the soul.

Thoughts about my faith being tested became an important part of taking myself to another level. Working through them helped me climb out of my moment of despair.

As I drove farther down the highway, I recalled the faces of our employees I had just left behind. Their fate and that of Texas Nameplate had not been written in stone. The judgment about our application's conformance with the Baldrige criteria was not like some modern version of the Ten Commandments.

After all, to a man and to a woman, we each still loved God with our whole heart, mind, soul, and spirit, and loved our neighbors as ourselves. We had not lost our way to that which counted the most.

What's more we still had each other and we still had a thriving business together. Through the quest for quality, we had rediscovered the old process of serving each other, no longer as master and servants, but as friends.

And as I left the highway and turned east into the town of Italy, it dawned on me what this whole process was all about.

There before me was a symbol of it staring me right in the face. I was passing a beautiful new home on the outskirts of Italy. It was my parents' new farm.

They had been called on to sacrifice the farm they had built in Waxahachie, for the good of all Americans. The federal government had taken their farm in 1990 for the science project called the Super-Collider. It was a project that was aimed at strengthening America and my parents had been a part of that historic venture.

What had taken them over 20 years to build had been taken from them in a day, for the sake of us all. As their new home showed everyone, they survived the taking, even though the ill-fated project unfortunately didn't.

In the case of Texas Nameplate, from the very first day of our quest, when it seemed that General Dynamics was effectively trying to take away our business, they were really trying to help us keep up with the pace of progress.

To stay in the competitive marketplace, what they saw and what we had to learn was the need for commitment to providing quality products and services. It would require many sacrifices for the good of all of us.

Like wise ones who knew what we needed before we did, they were really acting in our best interests even though we didn't know it at first. What we had originally seen as an attempt to drive us out of the marketplace was their attempt to keep us in it.

As I looked back at my parents' home in the rear-view mirror, I realized that the best thing about losing the Malcolm Baldrige Award this year was that we would get another chance to try for it the next year. With the feedback we got from the application process, we would be able to take the information, plug it into our strategic plan for 1998 and again improve Texas Nameplate. What's more, we could apply again in 1998 and get even more feedback if we lost again.

As I made my turn onto the narrow road leading to my farm, I was beginning to see the silver lining in the clouds.

That narrow road is an old country road. It sometimes reminds me of Mom and Dad. For a long time it has needed a little work after its many years of service, just like I often thought they did. Maybe they could have praised me more, maybe coached me more, maybe shown me their love more.

But it is very easy to be critical about how others live their lives, especially when it comes to our parents. Whatever their "failures," they had taught me to take ownership of my life, just as I was trying my best with Julie to teach our own two sons.

But if I learned anything along the roads I had taken in life, one of the most important things was surely to learn to forgive my parents as many times or more than they had forgiven me. I am sure that somewhere along the road, my sons may say a lot about my wrongdoings, my lacks, and they will doubtless be right in many ways. I hope they will forgive me.

As I made the last turn west to take the bridge over the highway, I could see my own farm in the distance. I thought about how parents can do just so much for their children. As my parents had done for me, Julie and I were now trying to do the best we could for our children. For the Crownover families, that always meant trying to be both happy and successful.

meant trying to be both happy and successful.

Turning into my driveway, my boys came running off the baseball field I had built for them and Julie walked out of the home where we got married. When I stepped out of the car, I finally found the words I was looking for to tell them about the real meaning of what had taken place on our quest for quality and the Malcolm Baldrige Award. But just as my words alone could never tell them how much I loved each of them, I knew it would likely be years before they fully understood what I had in my heart to say.

What I wanted to say was that, like Dad and Mom had given me, indeed like America gives to all of us, the most important thing about our journey was the opportunity to compete. It is the essence of American business. It is an American birthright just as much as any other and just as available to those who adopt America as home in fact or in spirit.

Looking into their eyes when my family came up to me, I knew that if our company had not competed, we would not have been faithful to what we had inherited from our fathers and mothers.

I now felt I was finally able to decide the issue my friends at General Dynamics had put to us:

**Will we change the way
we do business with each other
to achieve better quality?**

Yes, we will always be willing to change the way we do business to achieve better quality.

Greeting my family, I knew in my heart that the next generation of Crownovers will continue to compete and show Mr. Baldrige, and Whoever else may be watching over us all, how much we value our freedom to do so.

But I also knew in my heart, as we all gave each other welcoming hugs and kisses, that the words I wanted to say were best left unspoken for the moment. I would let my silence work on the words for their telling on some other days ...

Days when I could write this book from my heart ...

Days when they and other Crownovers could take heart in them ...

Days when they would, themselves, take the quest to the next level.

Robert Hodge, Jr.
Supervisor, Press Department

The Next Generation
"What brought me here was my father, Reverend Robert Hodge, Sr. He worked here ten years before I started. I worked during the summers in high school before I got hired full-time here at age 16 as the porter, sweeping the floor and cleaning out trashcans. The next year I scraped flats in the paint department. Then after graduation I worked in the press department as a shear operator full-time and have been here ever since, 18 years. After a couple of years I kept advancing. I eventually became assistant supervisor and later supervisor in etch and now in the press department."

Just DOIT
"Now I'm on the DOIT team (Daily Operations Innovation Team) with the other supervisors. We run the business in terms of daily operations. We share all our information with each other, with handouts, every two weeks in a meeting. It's amazing some of the charts and graphs we share with each other since we each have our own PC now. We make decisions and solve problems."

We Celebrate Each Other
"I've always enjoyed the people and the environment and the type of work we do here. That's what keeps me here. I just enjoy the way people get along with one another, communi-

cate, and help each other. The company does a lot to make everyone feel good when they come to work. We look forward to gainsharing and profit sharing, but also to a lot of picnics, Zero-Defect Day, company-sponsored dinners, group meetings every month, cake for all employees' birthdays, a Christmas party, a Halloween party. Celebrating with each other keeps us motivated."

Walk the Talk
"Dale comes around and talks to people. He's concerned not just about their work here but also about what's happening outside the job. He wants to know what everyone is doing in life. It makes us feel good that he's concerned about our families, makes us feel real special. Since Mr. 'C', Dale and I all live in Italy, we often sit down and talk awhile about what's happening in our town."

Highlights of the Quality Journey
"When we started into this quality journey, I was an assistant supervisor. Dale got the supervisors and later the assistant supervisors to take the SPC courses. That made everybody feel a part of it. We could see he was making changes for the better of the company and the people.

"Our first Z-D Day made everybody feel real special. They'd really worked hard and accomplished something for the company and for themselves too. After we won the Texas Quality Award, everyone felt really good and really close to one another. We knew Dale had done something to secure the future of the company and everyone in it. We'd taken the next step."

Taking It to the Next Level

"Since we started quality down here, it helps me look at my home life. Dale always told me that it would influence how I deal with my wife, my kids, and how we organize things in our house, community and church.

"I'm a deacon and a Sunday school teacher. In the community, I coach and referee basketball and I umpire baseball and softball. I stay busy all the time. I like to help kids in the community and at the church. You see, I'm a Christian man. I live life so that people can see I am a Christian. I work with a lot of people who aren't Christian. I have new ways now to work with them.

"So I try to take this home and get everyone else to follow and change and see what I'm trying to accomplish. It has opened me up even more to talking with people and has given me ideas I can use at home, in church and in my community."

EPILOGUE

Toward the end of 1997, I was again invited to attend the ceremonies in Washington, D.C. for the winners of the Malcolm Baldrige National Quality Award. I accepted.

As before, the ceremonies were really cool, very inspiring, and topped off by the President of the United States addressing us all.

During my visit in Washington, I had the opportunity to meet past and present Baldrige winners. To this day, I still have contact with them any time I need help.

I also met with four of the members of the Baldrige site-visit team who had come down to see Texas Nameplate. Even though they were unable to talk specifically about our application, they encouraged us to try it again. I told them we were planning to.

Late in May 1998, Texas Nameplate Company submitted its third application and entered the competition for the 1998 Malcolm Baldrige National Quality Award. As we go to press with this story of our quest for quality, we await this year's judgment.

A Final Meditation

Whenever I visit Washington, D.C., and I walk among the most powerful of men and women there, I am reminded of the example Jesus set for leaders:

From *John 13: 12–15*

"After he had washed their feet, he asked them, 'Do you know what I have done to you? You call me Teacher and Lord – and you are right, for that is what I am. So if I, your Lord and Teacher, have washed your feet, you also ought to wash one another's feet. For I have set you an example, that you also should do as I have done to you."

In America, the land of the free, we would be well-advised to treat others as friends, even when competing in the marketplace.

From *John 15: 12–15*

"This is my commandment, that you love one another as I have loved you. No one has greater love than this, to lay down their life for one's friends. You are my friends if you do what I command you. I do not call you slaves any longer, because the slave does not know what the master is doing; but I have called you friends, because I have made known to you everything that I have heard from my Father."

Appendix

Glossary

- **Benchmarking**—setting goals based on results already achieved by world leaders in similar activities; gathering data to compare one's performance to an industry's best.

- **Crosby School**—founded by Philip B. Crosby, located in Winter Park, Florida, the school teaches leaders how to implement a total quality approach to business.

- **Drivers**—driving forces that influence an organization's decision making and strategic planning.

- **Gainsharing**—a compensation incentive that rewards employees for doing it right the first time by sharing gains in productivity.

- **ISO 9000**—International Organization for Standardizations. A series of standards that define quality management and quality system elements and guidelines.

- **Malcolm Baldrige National Quality Award**—the Malcolm Baldrige National Quality Improvement Act of 1987, signed by President Reagan established this annual competition to promote an understanding of the requirements for performance excellence and competitiveness improvements and to promote sharing of information on successful performance strategies. Awarded by the Secretary of Commerce, it is the most prestigious quality award in the U.S.

- **Nonconformances**—defects in manufactured parts, not meeting specifications.

- **Quest**—annual ceremony in Washington, D.C. to inspire competition for the Malcolm

Baldrige National Quality Award.

- **QIT**—quality improvement team. A group of employees chartered to discover causes, develop and implement remedies, and measure quality improvements.
- **Site visit**—equates to semi-finalist. A team of examiners visits the applicant's premises to audit the company's systems and processes and to verify results reported in the award application.
- **SPC**—statistical process control. A body of statistical techniques used to measure and monitor the performance of a process.
- **Texas Quality Award**—state-held competition for quality administered by Texas Quality Foundation, Austin, Texas.
- **TQM**—total quality management. A structured management process linking all of a company's systems and processes to ensure that all the goods and services provided serve the purpose of delighting customers.
- **World-class**—a descriptive term used to denote best in the world when describing a practice or process or company. Any company achieving 867 points out of 1000 in the Malcolm Baldrige results can be benchmarked as world-class.
- **Zero defects**—an attitude or a philosophy of preventing errors, of doing things right the first time, popularized by Philip B. Crosby.
- **Z-D Day**—a day of celebration of the entire company's commitment to zero defects.

HIGH PROFILE: DALE CROWNOVER

- **My name is** Dale Crownover.
- **My e-mail address is** dale@nameplate.com
- **I am involved in the following community activities:** Texas Quality Award Board of Directors, Texas Association of Business and Chambers of Commerce Board of Directors, South Dallas Development Corp.
- **My occupation is** President, Texas Nameplate Company, Inc.
- **My birth place** is Dallas, TX.
- **My family consists of** my wife Julie, my two sons, Ryan and Dan, my dog Charlie, and nine cows.
- **My hobbies include** farming and golf.
- **If I had a different job, I'd be a** jet pilot.
- **My favorite trademark expression is** "let's take it to the next level."
- **My best habit is** being at home every night before my kids go to bed.
- **My favorite junk food is** double-meat cheeseburgers and French fries.
- **For my last meal, I would choose** rib-eye steak, baked potato, and a Caesar salad.
- **My favorite possession is** my college graduation ring.
- **The electrical device I can't live without is** hedge clippers.
- **I drive a** Mercedes Benz.
- **If I could, I'd drive** my John Deere tractor.

- **My all-time favorite movie is** *The Great Escape.*
- **My all-time favorite television program is** "Hee Haw."
- **Nobody knows** I try to please everyone.
- **My teenage idol was** Roger Staubach.
- **My favorite magazine is** *Farm Journal.*
- **The last book I read was** *Total Quality Management* by Stephen George and Arnold Weimerskirch.
- **My ideal vacation is** going to Hawaii with my family.
- **The biggest honor I've ever received is** our company being named recipient of the Texas Quality Award.
- **I regret** not getting to know my grandfather better.
- **I'm tired of** lazy people.
- **The biggest waste of time is** waiting in line.
- **The best use of time is** being at work and being productive.
- **The four guests at my fantasy dinner party would be** Tom Landry; my grandfather; my grandmother; and my uncle, R. B. Ewing.
- **I'm happiest when** my family and employees are happy.

THE QUALITY LEADERS

Meet the Quality Leaders
at Texas Nameplate!

The people you see pictured on the following pages are proud to produce nameplates in an award-winning, quality manner. You'll meet members of each department, members of the Crownover family, and share special moments in the company's recent history. Enjoy your tour!

Texas Nameplate Company, Inc. founded in 1946, manufacturers of etched and screened products, is located at 1900 South Ervay Street, Dallas, Texas.

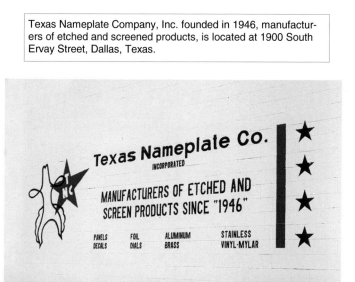

Two generations of Crownovers lead Texas Nameplate Company: Roy Crownover (left), Founder and CEO, and son Dale Crownover, President.

Bob Mantle, Sales Manager (left), and Kris Foster, Inside Sales, sell nameplate solutions to TNC's international clientele.

Larry Goldman (right) and Kim Schweitzer, Outside Sales, tour the country visiting customers and prospects.

Kenny Howard, Customer Service Manager, Ginger Howard (middle), and Debra Shelby interact with customers to take orders and ensure customer satisfaction.

Preston Smith (left), Production Manager, LaDonna Norris, Pre-Production, and Jimmy Spurger, Pre-Production Manager (right) assure that information received from customers is accurate as TNC prepares to produce the product.

Julian Ramirez (left), Connie Banks (middle), Art Department Supervisor, and Betty Bartos turn schematics or drawings from the customer into artwork. They design on computer and transfer the information onto film.

Verdie Jones, Expedite Team Leader, ensures efficient production workflow by coordinating the efforts of multiple-purpose employees.

11th Street facility (back row left to right): Ronnie Phelps, Screen Supervisor, Rayann Moore, Lucky Ortega, David Norris, Production Manager, (front row left to right) Jaime De La Paz, Leticia Retiz, Yolanda Pacheco, and Bonnie Reese produce the non-metal nameplates using synthetic lexans, vinyls, polycarbonates, and mylars.

Weldon Bounds cuts the metal sheets into 20" by 24" flats.

Ernest Burleson (right), Tool & Die Supervisor, and Sidney Hib-bitt, Sr. are the master craftsmen who supply the tools and dies that accurately punch holes in the nameplates. The process is like sculpting ½" thick steel, truly a work of art.

Screen Department (left to right): Enrique Ramirez, Otto Adams, Tim Jacob, Mike Martinez, Robert Brown, Supervisor and Ruby Reese (seated), take the film and expose it onto the screen, from which the image is printed on cut metal flats.

Etch Department (left to right): Roger Walker and Mario Amezcua run the metal flats through an etch machine to etch nameplate designs to depths measured in 1/1000th of an inch.

Paint Department (left to right): Fernando Rojas, Jerry Wilson, Roque Lopez and Larry Johnson, Supervisor (not shown) apply lacquer to metal flats according to customers' color requirements, bake the flats for 20 minutes to cure the ink, then strip the excess paint.

Press Department (back row left to right): Homero Garcia, Robert Hodge, Jr., Supervisor, Greg Odom, Herberto Candido, Sr., Noel Gomez, Debra Thompson, (front row left to right) Willie Mae Moore, Martha De La Fuenta, and Rosa Valdez run the machinery that cuts and punches individual nameplates from the metal flats.

Shipping Department (back row left to right): Candies Key, Rodney Gonzales, Reverend Robert Hodge, Sr., Natalia Gomez, (front row left to right) Carolyn Howard, Sandra Lazaro, and Carol Avila, Supervisor, need only weigh the nameplates to fill an order, so accurate is the process to this point.

Maintenance Department (right to left): Adolfo Pena and Bonnie Perez keep the facility and grounds in spotless, working condition.

Troy Knowlton, Operations Manager, proudly displays the rich variety of nameplates produced.

Sula Reilly, Human Resource Advocate, updates the Quality Corner charts and graphs daily.

Customer Accounts: Margaret Rose (left) and Brenda Falcon handle accounts receivable and other financial processes.

Scott Weber, Director of Administration, leads the finance and administration team.

R. B. Ewing, TNC's Quality Control Manager for decades and Dale's uncle, died in 1995.

Ranga Kambhampaty taught quality business processes to Dale in 1994. Ranga died in 1995.

Texas Nameplate Company received the Texas Quality Award in 1996, the year the company celebrated its 50th anniversary.

Dale graduated with a Bachelor of Science degree in Business Management from LeTourneau University in 1997.

Texas Nameplate Company received the Arthur Andersen Best Practices Award in 1997.

Dale and Julie Crownover were married at home on July 5, 1988.

Bernyce Crownover (left), Dale's mother, and Julie Crownover, Dale's wife, provide wisdom, inspiration, and encouragement.

Ryan and Dan Crownover, the next generation, greet their dad returning home to the farm, as their mom looks on.

THE PLAYERS WHO TAKE IT TO THE NEXT LEVEL

Family
Roy Crownover
Bernyce Crownover
Dale Crownover
Julie Crownover
Dan and Ryan Crownover

Employees
Adolfo Pena
Betty Bartos
Bob Mantle
Bonifacia Perez
Brenda Falcon
Candies Key
Carol Avila
Carolyn Howard
Connie Banks
David Norris
Debra Shelby
Debra Thompson
Diana Casablanca
Enrique Ramirez
Ernest Burleson
Fernando Rojas
Ginger Howard
Greg Odom
Herberto Candido, Sr.

Homero Garcia
Jaime De La Paz
Jerry Wilson
Jimmy Spurger
Julian Ramirez
Kenny Howard
Kim Schweitzer
Kris Foster
LaDonna Norris
Larry Goldman
Larry Johnson
Letitia Retiz
Lucky Ortega
Margaret Rose
Mario Amezcua
Martha De La Fuente
Mike Martinez
Natalia Gomez
Noel Gomez
Otto Adams
Preston Smith, Jr.
Rayann Moore
Robert Brown
Robert Hodge, Jr.
Robert Hodge, Sr.
Rodney Gonzales
Roger Walker
Ronnie Phelps
Roque Lopez
Rosa Marie Valdez
Ruby Reese
Sandra Lazaro
Scott Weber
Sidney Hibbitt, Sr.
Sula Reilly

Tim Jacob
Troy Knowlton
Verdie Lee Jones
Weldon Bounds
Willie Mae Moore
Yolanda Morse

Colleagues
Barry Johnson
Bruce Beede
Glenn Bodinson
Jackie Kennett
Larry Cameron
Steve Barrett
Warren Hogan

Bibliography

AMA Management Handbook, edited by John J. Hampton

BrainStyles: Change Your Life Without Changing Who You Are, by Marlane Miller

Lincoln on Leadership: Leadership Strategies for Tough Times, by Donald Phillips

Quality Is Free: The Art of Making Quality Certain, by Philip B. Crosby

Quality Without Tears, by Philip B. Crosby

The Leadership Challenge: How to Get Extraordinary Things Done in Your Organization, by James Kouzes and Barry Posner

The ISO 9000 Book, by John T. Rabbitt and Peter A. Bergh

Total Quality Management, by Stephen George and Arnold Weimerskirch

CREDITS

Special Thanks to:

- **David Branch, Daniel Hanson, Robin Berryman, Susie Long, Myra Stockner, Fred Herbert,** and **Joe Trussell** of Branch Smith Printing, Inc., our partners in the quality production of the book.
- **Kris Hundt** for the series of photographs that introduce our Texas Nameplate Players to you.
- **LaDonna Norris** and **Kenny Howard** of Texas Nameplate Company for hosting our many visits to the facility.
- **Tammy Hevia, Peg Thomas,** and **Vic Sassone** of the Hogan Center for their project support.
- **Mary Bold** of the Association of Independent Book Publishers and **Pam Lange** of Book Publishers of Texas for their guidance and wise counsel.
- **All of our wonderful colleagues, family members and friends** who read the manuscript, provided invaluable feedback, and encouraged our hearts.

ABOUT
LINDA BUSH AND JOHN DARROUZET

Linda Bush and John Darrouzet are creative, passionate visionaries who believe the future belongs to those who learn deeply how to make decisions. No more. No less.

Linda is a master facilitator and curriculum developer with an international consulting practice. John is an accomplished lawyer, a software engineer, and a successful writer.

With over 50 years of combined experience, they coach others to master the process of decision making by helping leaders:

- Gain perspective on their ordinary worlds
- Focus on real issues
- Turn reluctance into commitment
- Realize the wisdom of crisis
- Confront the "bad news" with "good news"
- Address the "Powers That Be"
- Find significance in personal reflection
- Marshall facts and reasons
- Discover inspiring insights and oversights
- Tell their compelling stories
- Anticipate objections
- Present decisions with conviction.

For more information, please contact them at:
Deciders@aol.com

ABOUT
THE HOGAN CENTER

**Helping Companies
Achieve Performance Excellence**

The Hogan Center for Performance Excellence is dedicated to helping organizations and individuals achieve higher levels of performance in all aspects of their businesses, from increasing sales and market share, to improved profits and return on investment. In short, we want to help your organization attain a sustained competitive advantage in your marketplace. By combining the resources of many companies such as yours, we are able to offer affordable, result-oriented services to companies of all sizes.

We have a permanent staff and associates of more that two dozen experts in a wide variety of business-related fields, from strategic planning, to ISO registration, to accelerated adult learning. Our Learning Center is located in Dallas, Texas. Our associates, and our community of customers, are located throughout the United States.

Our History

Founded in 1987 by Warren Hogan, the Hogan Center was begun in response to a call for help from a dozen small companies who wanted to significantly improve their performance.

The consortium concept proved enormously successful. Under Hogan's guidance and leadership, this concept has grown and matured into the Two-Year Transformation program. Since 1987, more than 120 companies have completed the two-year program.

The Hogan Center continued to grow as our customers asked for a variety of additional services. In 1988, we began providing consulting services to help companies improve targeted areas of operational and management systems. In 1989, the Executive Roundtable was started for companies who are well along the journey towards performance excellence.

In 1992, Hogan expanded the Center's services by providing public seminars for companies who needed on-going training for their workforce. In 1994, the Center began offering organizational assessments and employee satisfaction surveys to help member companies quickly identify areas for improvement.

In 1995, we started the Learning Center to better focus our efforts in researching best practices in performance enhancement and accelerated learning. One result of this research is the Quest for Improved Performance program which was started in 1996 to provide a more structured forum for graduates from the two-year consortium program.

Today, the Hogan Center offers a full range of

consortium, training and consulting services to
help companies achieve their performance
goals.

Outstanding Results

A great many of our members have achieved
outstanding performance as a result of incorpo-
rating the Hogan Center approaches into their
daily business practices. Over the years, many
of our members have been honored for their
achievements. Marlow Industries was honored
in 1991 with the Malcolm Baldrige National
Quality Award. Both M&S Systems and Texas
Nameplate received the 1996 Texas Quality
Award. John Deere Dallas Branch received the
1997 Texas Quality Award, TDIndustries won
in 1998.

The Hogan Center is dedicated to strengthening
America. We help organizations, teams and individuals achieve performance excellence. Our
clients use the Hogan Center's implementation
training and support services to achieve market,
operational, and financial superiority.

Performance Enhancement Programs

Our consortium programs provide organizations
an affordable resource for gaining significantly
improved performance. We offer three levels of
membership:

•The Two-Year Transformation program is for

organizations who want to implement the basic systems and methods for high performance.

•Quest for Improved Performance is a structured program for organizations who want to build on basics to accelerate performance improvements.

•The Executive Roundtable is a monthly venue for more advanced organizations who want an affordable source of strategic information, networking, and benchmarking.

Organizational Effectiveness Services

Our consulting services provide targeted interventions to help organizations complete strategic-level projects or to implement key systems and methods. These services are for organizations who want to accelerate improvements in key areas. Our services include:

•Organization Assessments
•Process Management
•Leadership Systems
•Benchmarking
•Strategic Planning
•ISO 9000
•Measurement Systems
•Award Applications

People Effectiveness Services

Our public seminars concentrate on improving

the leadership and management skills of employees at all levels of the organization. Our workshops are designed for interactive, accelerated learning to help your employees quickly master key skills. We offer all seminars and workshops through both public and private classes:

- Practical Skills for Managers
- Leadership Skills for Executives/Managers
- Interview Skills for Managers
- Finance for the Non-Financial Professional
- Managing Team Relationships
- Tools for Team Leaders

The Learning Center

Our Learning Center is the focal point for learning and adapting world-class methods and tools for performance excellence to the needs of small to medium-sized companies. We offer a full range of membership programs and services through the Learning Center.

The Hogan Center for Performance Excellence provides a comprehensive array of seminar programs designed to enhance the skills of executives, managers, supervisors, team leaders and teams.

Practical Skills
for Managers and Supervisors
A practical three-day program, designed to give new or experienced managers and supervisors

practical, basic skills for handling day-to-day employee interactions.

Finance / Accounting for the Non-Financial Professional

An intensive one-day program, designed to enable non-financial professionals to understand financial reports and decision making based on the financial performance of your organization.

Interview Skills for Managers

An intensive one-day program, designed to equip managers, supervisors, and human resource coordinators with enhanced skills for interviewing and hiring the right person the first time.

Leadership Skills for Executives

A transforming four-day program designed to enable senior executives to develop enhanced leadership practices needed to motivate and energize today's empowered workforce.

Leadership Skills for Managers

A transforming four-day program designed to enable managers and supervisors to develop enhanced leadership practices needed to motivate and energize today's empowered workforce.

Managing Team Relationships

This one-day program is designed to help team leaders, facilitators, and coaches understand and effectively manage the dynamics of human relationships in teams.

Quality Leadership & Implementation

An intensive two-day executive seminar in the benefits, core-values, and strategies of managing for performance excellence.

Tools for Team Leadership

This one-day program provides training and practice in proven tools and techniques for leading and facilitating team meetings.

Introduction to Statistical Process Control

For an organization to succeed in today's highly competitive environment, the use of tools to solve problems, improve performance, and sustain performance is a must. These tools must be introduced in simple and easy to understand language so that everyone in the organization can assimilate and use them. This "Introduction to Statistical Process Control" workshop has been designed in every day language so that these powerful tools may be used immediately in the organization.

For more information, please contact us at:

The Hogan Center for Performance Excellence
2915 LBJ Freeway, Suite 152
Dallas, Texas 75234-7607
e-mail: warren@hogancenter.com
Website: www.hogancenter.com

What's the Next Level for You?

We sincerely hope this story has inspired you to reflect on your own personal or business quest for quality.

As we continue to learn, to grow and to give, we offer to facilitate an open dialogue. We encourage you to participate in this learning community by sharing with us your thoughts, ideas, questions, and feedback. As learning partners in the quest, we can all take it to the next level.

Please write to us at:

NextLevel Press
c/o The Hogan Center
for Performance Excellence
2915 LBJ Freeway
Suite 152
Dallas, Texas 75234

Or send e-mail to:

Dale Crownover: dale@nameplate.com
Linda Bush & John Darrouzet:
Deciders@aol.com
Warren Hogan: warren@hogancenter.com

We look forward to hearing from you!